WOODWORKER'S
POCKET
REFERENCE

EVERYTHING A WOODWORKER NEEDS TO KNOW AT A GLANCE *Second Edition*

CHARLIE SELF

FOX CHAPEL
PUBLISHING

© 2005, 2014 by Charlie Self and Fox Chapel Publishing Company, Inc.,
903 Square Street, Mount Joy, PA 17552.

Woodworker's Pocket Reference, Second Edition (2014) is a revised edition of *Woodworker's Pocket Reference* (2005), published by Fox Chapel Publishing Company, Inc. Revisions include new content.

ISBN 978-1-56523-811-4

Library of Congress Cataloging-in-Publication Data

Self, Charles R.
  Woodworker's pocket reference / Charlie Self. -- Second edition.
      pages cm
  Includes index.
  ISBN 978-1-56523-811-4
  1. Woodwork--Handbooks, manuals, etc. I. Title. II. Title: Do-it-yourself pocket guide.
  TT180.S39798 2014
  684'.08--dc23
                                    2013018329

To learn more about the other great books from Fox Chapel Publishing, or to find a retailer near you, call toll-free 800-457-9112 or visit us at *www.FoxChapelPublishing.com*.

We are always looking for talented authors. To submit an idea, please send a brief inquiry to acquisitions@foxchapelpublishing.com.

Printed in the USA

Table of Contents

About the Author

Woodworker Charlie Self is an award-winning writer who has contributed a vast amount of work to the woodworking field. He has won the 2002 Vaughan-Bushnell Golden Hammer Award for his feature article in *Woodworker's Journal*, the 2001 Vaughan-Bushnell Award for best feature article for his work in *Woodworker's Journal*, the 2000 Vaughan-Bushnell DIY best feature article award for his work in *Digital Home* (Smart Computing), and the 1994 annual Stanley Awards DIY for books for *Woodworker's Source Book* (Betterway, 1993). Formerly a senior writer for Woodcraft Supply Corp., Charlie wrote over 40 articles and two dozen newsletter introductions. Along with his article work at Woodcraft, he also created the Woodworker of the Month feature. Charlie has written many books, including *Cabinets and Countertops*, *Woodworker's Guide to Selecting & Milling Wood*, *Creating Your Own Woodworking Shop*, and *Building Your Own Home*, and has written over 1,000 articles for publications such as *Popular Woodworking*, *Wood Carving Illustrated*, *Woodshop News*, and *Woodworker's Journal*. He has also edited and consulted for companies such as DeWalt, Grizzly Industrial, McGraw-Hill, Time-Life, and Popular Mechanics Encyclopedia. Charlie enjoys updating his blog at http://charlie-self.blogspot.com/.

CHAPTER 1

Selecting & Working Common Woods

Wood is a superb material with many uses. Pleasing to the eye, it is easily worked and shaped. It lasts a long time and takes a fine finish. It can also be colored as desired, with stains or paints.

Plywood

Plywood is usually made up of an odd number of plies. Face plies have the grain running the long way of the panel and intermediate plies running in opposing directions. The plies running in different directions make plywood more dimensionally stable than solid wood.

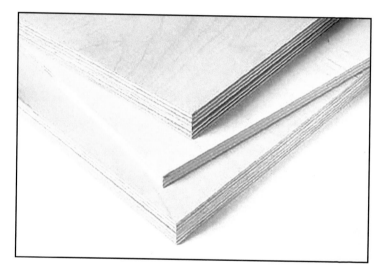

With plywood, wide-panel faces do not warp or cup. Plywood is also useful as backs, sides, and bottoms for desks, cabinets, and other projects where those parts are not seen. It may also be used as a substrate for laminates and veneers. Plywood is also available in a huge range of wood veneers, including walnut, cherry, hickory, and much more.

SELECTING & WORKING COMMON WOODS

Depending on your project, plywood may be just what you need. For example, if you're building your own kitchen cabinets, the bulk of the material will be plywood. I use a pre-finished maple plywood that eliminates a lot of tedious labor and is quite beautiful as well. In a case like this, you'll be building lots of boxes and then crafting the doors out of solid wood, plywood, or a combination of both. If you plan to build reproduction

furniture, plywood won't figure in, but if you'd like to build sturdy, inexpensive shelving units for your home, then plywood is a great choice. I've built a lot of storage pieces that are essentially "cases on bases," which is another way of saying that they are simple plywood boxes that are elevated on stylish hardwood bases and outfitted with drawers and doors as needed.

A case on base piece.

Tip: A common concern with plywood is handling the 4' x 8' sheets that it comes in, especially if you don't have a truck or van. Most lumberyards and home centers, however, will rip the sheets to whatever size you specify, often at no additional charge. This invaluable service can save both time and hassle.

If you choose to integrate plywood into your designs, you'll need to consider how to treat its edge. Most people cover the edges with hardwood strips that they glue on and then sand flush, or use some kind of glue-on edge tape. This latter method is easy and inexpensive—the tape comes in rolls of various lengths and is simply ironed on. This activates the glue on the underside of the tape, and the excess can easily be trimmed off. Edge tape can tend to peel up over time if it isn't carefully stuck down, however, so make sure to hone your technique on some scrap stock.

Softwood Plywood Grades

- **Grade A** is smooth, free of knots, pitch pockets, open splits, and open defects. Synthetic filler fills cracks and checks.
- **Grade B** is solid, free of open defects and broken grain. Slightly rough grain is OK. Minor sanding and patching defects in up to 5% of the panel.
- **Grade C** plywood is underlayment for wood floors or sheathing.
- **Grade D** is a backer veneer in CDX (a low grade of construction plywood) and a filler ply in other plywoods.
- **Softwood plywoods** come in combinations: A-A and A-B; B-B and B-C.
- **Overlaid plywoods** serve as desktops with a smooth finish for glossy paints.
- **Medium-Density Overlay** is an Exterior grade (with waterproof glue), and is available in Marine grade as well, in B-B, with inner plies at least C grade. The overlay is resin on fiber for a smooth, uniform surface. Overlay thickness is at least 0.012" thick.
- **High-Density** Overlay resin contains more solids than those used in MDO.

Oriented Strand Board

Oriented Strand Board (OSB) uses strands of wood, formed with resins into a panel in standard panel sizes and thicknesses. Heat and pressure are used.

Tempered OSB is used as pegboard and backer boards for cabinets and low-end bookshelves. Available in from 2' x 2' to 4' x 8' panels.

Particle Boards

A variety of grades and sizes of particle boards exist.

Countertop grade is used by cabinetmakers as underlayment for laminates on kitchen counters and other surfaces. Some types are susceptible to water damage, but moisture-resistant MDF is available. Both are available in a variety of sheet sizes from 4' x 8' to materials as much as 147" long. The long sheets are for countertop use. MDF is also the core for much hardwood plywood, and the core stock in much melamine. Melamine (plastic) is fused to the top and bottom of the particle board, forming a surfaced board for shelving.

MDF (Medium-Density Fiberboard) is a popular product for furniture and cabinet construction. It is made of smaller pieces of wood than regular particle board for finer grading and provides a smoother surface for thin laminates such as veneers. Water-resistant varieties are available.

Hardwood Plywoods

Hardwood plywoods' dimensional stability and speed of construction are positives. Crossbanded plies are laid at 90° to each other. Interior plies are softwood or a very low grade of hardwood (tulip poplar is popular). **MDF core** is stable, less expensive, very heavy, and doesn't hold screws well. It is often all you can find in a particular face veneer. **Lumber core** has a solid wood core and two or more crossband veneers. **All-veneer** has face and back veneer, crossband veneers, and a veneer core. Strength is closer to uniform across the face grain due to crossbanding.

Thickness: ⅛", ¼", ⅜", ½", and ¾", with ⁷⁄₁₆", ⅝", ⅞", 1", and 1¼" available on special order. Metric sizes are also available.

Standard sheets: 4' x 8'. Other sizes: 2' x 2', 2' x 4', 4' x 4', 4' x 6', 4' x 10', and 5' x 8'.

Color and grain match in premium grades.
Baltic birch is stronger than American, but more costly.

CHAPTER 1

Bending plywood is made with special adhesives that are more flexible, in thicknesses from ⅛" to ⅜". Thicker bending plywoods have a kerfed core (slotted along the radius that is to be bent) to allow easier bending without a need to build up several thinner pieces.

Veneer Matching

Book Match—like opened pages of a book, with identical opposite patterns.

Slip Match—progressive pieces of veneer side-by-side.

Whole Piece—single pieces of veneer.

Pleasing Match—face veneer matched for color, but not for figure characteristics.

Mismatch or Random Match—veneer pieces joined to create an unmatched effect.

Unmatched—no attention to figure, color, or uniformity, for project backs.

Characteristics of Wood

It's important to consider the many characteristics of wood when selecting the appropriate species for your project. These characteristics include:

- appearance (grain, figure, and color)
- weight and strength
- workability
- ease of gluing
- ease of fastening

- durability
- ease of bending
- movement
- ease of smoothing
- acceptance of stains

Appearance

Grain, color, and figure are wood's top features.

Grain, or the direction of the wood fibers, varies from straight grain, which runs straight along the length of the board, to irregular grain, which twists and turns in different directions. Common grain types are:

- Straight—runs parallel to length of tree
- Cross—doesn't runs parallel to length of tree
- Interlocked—forms alternating left- and right-hand spirals
- Spiral—runs in spirals
- Wavy—runs in repeating waves
- Curly—runs in irregular waves
- Irregular—twists and turns in different directions
- Diagonal—runs diagonally across the board

Wood colors vary from the bright white of holly to the dark olive of greenheart to the black of ebony. Color variations within a single board can create such complex patterns that appearance problems may arise for the novice woodworker during the assembly. Many highly colored woods change color, even indoors. For example, cherry darkens as it ages and is exposed to light; walnut lightens; purpleheart and redheart fade to a brown color over time. Much color change can be reduced by using a UV (ultraviolet) resistant finish.

Figures are numerous and often result from the wood's grain type. For instance, bird's eye figure is often seen as a result of a curly grain. Generally, quarter-sawn (QS) lumber shows more interesting figures than does flat sawn, with rays and ribbon stripes being common in quarter-sawn lumber.

Weight and Strength

Weight and strength are very closely related. Heavier, denser woods are often the strongest and the most able to absorb shock.

Workability

Hardness, grain, and density all affect the workability of the wood. Generally, woods that are softer, have a straighter grain, and are more dense are easiest to work.

Durability—A wood's durability relates to its natural ability to resist decay, especially when placed in the ground or in an environment where the wood is exposed to high amounts of moisture.

Ease of Bending—Bending can be done with or without steam. Some green woods—ash is an example—bend easily and retain their assumed shape when dried, while others break too easily. Hardwoods typically bend more easily than softwoods.

Ease of Smoothing—Smoothing is affected by wood's hardness, grain, and density. Softer, straighter grained, and denser woods are most easily smoothed.

Acceptance of Stains—A wood's acceptance of stains and finishes is greatly affected by the openness of the pores. The use of a pre-stain conditioner will help a stain to be absorbed more evenly when working with problem woods.

Movement

Movement indicates the degree the wood species might distort. The higher the movement, the more the wood is apt to distort. It is largely affected by the moisture content of wood. As the wood's moisture content raises or lowers, the wood swells and contracts. Almost all woods are more stable if they are quarter-sawn, but quarter-sawing also makes a drastic change in the appearance of many woods, bringing to light the medullary rays that are characteristic of that type of cut.

Understanding basic principles of wood movement is crucial in high quality woodworking. Essentially, wood expands and contracts across its width, but not along its length. The rule of thumb is to assume ¼" per foot of width, to be on the safe side. When you're dealing with a single, narrow board, the degree of movement may be negligible, but if you've glued together a series of boards, you'll need to proceed carefully. For example, if you have a tabletop that is 3' wide, it could move as much as ¾" during the year. That means that you have to fasten this tabletop to its base in such a way that it is able to "float" in an unrestricted manner. If you simply screw it in place, it will either crack or warp dramatically.

Characteristics of Popular Woods

The wood examples shown here describe the highlights of woods that are popular and available to most woodworkers in our hemisphere, and a few woods that are harder to find but useful or fun to work.

*Asterisks mark those woods that cause irritation or sensitize. All wood is now classified as carcinogenic if you are overexposed to it, so we recommend that you always wear a dust mask.

Dollar signs $, $$, $$$, $$$$ are used to indicate whether a wood is low in cost ($), moderate ($$), expensive ($$$), or out-of-sight ($$$$).

Availability
● Wide availability
◗ Modest availability
○ Limited availability
◗ Hard to find

sp gr = specific gravity

Alder, red*

Pale pinkish-brown. Straight grain.

Weight/Strength: .41 sp gr. Medium
strength, stable.
Workability: Works easily. Accepts glue well,
holds fasteners well. Not durable. Finishes
well. Mimics cherry when stained.
Movement: Moderate.
Uses: Toys, carving, furniture.

Hardwood $ ●

Ash*

Light-brown. Straight grain.

Weight/Strength: .49 to .60 sp gr.
Strong, stable.
Workability: Works easily. Accepts glue
well, holds fasteners well. Excellent
steambending wood. Not durable.
Takes a high polish.
Movement: Moderate.
Uses: Fine furniture, tool handles.

Hardwood $ ●

Avodire*

Cream to pale-yellow. Irregularly
interlocked grain.

Weight/Strength: .48 sp gr. Strong, stable.
Workability: Works easily with hand and
power tools. Accepts glue well, screws
hold well. Use pilot holes to prevent
splitting. Not durable. Stains unevenly,
finishes well.
Movement: Low.
Uses: Furniture, veneers.

Hardwood $$$ ◗

Baldcypress

Yellow-brown to darker, red-brown.
Straight grain.

Weight/Strength: .42 sp gr. Medium
strength, stable.
Workability: Works easily. Accepts glue well,
holds screws and nails well. Durable.
Easily finished, including paint.
Movement: Moderate to low.
Uses: Outdoor projects.

Softwood $$ ●

Basswood

Creamy light-tan. Straight grain.

Weight/Strength: .37 sp gr. Low
strength, stable.
Workability: Soft, works easily. Accepts glue
well, holds detail for carving. Not durable.
Stains may blotch.
Movement: Moderate to low.
Uses: Patternmaking, handcarving, beehives.

Hardwood $ ●

Beech*

Pale-tan. Straight grain.

Weight/Strength: .64 sp gr. Strong,
medium stability.
Workability: Works easily. Accepts glue well,
holds fasteners well. Not durable. Stains
may blotch.
Movement: High.
Uses: Cabinetry, furniture, flooring, veneer.

Hardwood $$ ●

Selecting & Working Common Woods

Birch*

Pale-tan. Straight grain.

Weight/Strength: .55 to .65 sp gr.
Strong, stable.
Workability: Works easily. Accepts glue well,
holds fasteners well. Not durable. Stains
may blotch.
Movement: Low.
Uses: Cabinets, furniture, turnings, turned
toys, interior millwork.

Hardwood $$ ●

Bubinga*

Dark red-brown. Straight or interlocked grain.

Weight/Strength: .88 sp gr. Strong, stable.
Workability: Straight grain works easily
with sharp tools. Accepts glue well,
holds fasteners well. Durable. Stains well,
finishes beautifully.
Movement: Moderate to low.
Uses: Turnings, furniture parts,
decorative veneer.

Hardwood $$$ ○

Butternut

Light-brown. Straight grain.

Weight/Strength: .38 specific gravity.
Medium strength, stable.
Workability: Works very well. Accepts glue
well, holds fasteners well. Not durable.
Stains and finishes well; dark stain
resembles walnut.
Movement: Moderate to high.
Uses: Furniture, cabinetry, trim.

Hardwood $ ◗

Selecting & Working Common Woods

Cedar, Eastern Red*
Reddish color. Straight grain.

Weight/Strength: .47 specific gravity. Low strength, stable.
Workability: Works easily. Accepts glue well, holds fasteners well. Durable. Harder than western red cedar. Finishes well; may have pitch pockets.
Movement: Moderate.
Uses: Clothing containers, closet linings, small boxes, outdoor projects not needing great strength.

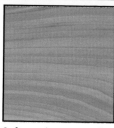

Softwood $ ●

Cedar, Western Red*
Reddish-brown. Straight grain, coarse texture.

Weight/Strength: .32 specific gravity. Low strength, stable.
Workability: Works easily. Accepts glue well, holds fasteners well. Durable. Finishes well.
Movement: High.
Uses: Outdoor projects, siding.

Hardwood $ ●

Cherry, Black
Red-brown, darkens with age. Straight grain.

Weight/Strength: .50 sp gr. Strong, stable.
Workability: Works easily. Burns at slow feed rate, demands sharp tools. Not durable. Finishes very well, beautiful luster.
Movement: Moderate.
Uses: Furniture, turnings, flooring (not for high traffic areas).

Hardwood $$ ●

Cocobolo*

Turns deep red with black stripes or mottling when exposed to air. Straight to interwoven grain.

Weight/Strength: Up to .98 sp gr. Careful seasoning needed for good stability.
Workability: Turns well. Difficult to glue because it is waxy. Durable. Low luster, finishes smoothly.
Movement: Moderate to low.
Uses: Handles, brush backs, jewelry boxes, chessmen, and other small pieces.

Hardwood $$$$ ○

Elm, American

Light-brown, sometimes reddish. Straight grain, often interlocked.

Weight/Strength: .63 sp gr. Strong, stable.
Workability: Works easily with sharp tools (power preferred). Accepts glue well, holds fasteners well. Excellent steam-bending wood. Durable. Finishes well.
Movement: Moderate to low.
Uses: Fine furniture, boxes, baskets.

Hardwood $$ ○

Goncalo Alves*

Russet or orange-brown, with irregular stripes of dark brown. Straight to interlocked to wavy grain, fine texture.

Weight/Strength: .97 sp gr. Strong, stable.
Workability: Works easily with power tools, interlocked grain is harder to work. Difficult to glue. Very durable. Takes clear finishes well.
Movement: Moderate once dried.
Uses: Small items, knife handles.

Hardwood $$$ ▶

Selecting & Working Common Woods

Hickory

Whitish heartwood. Straight grain, coarse texture.

Weight/Strength: .75 sp gr. Very strong, stable.
Workability: Hard to work, dulls tools quickly. Accepts glue well, holds fasteners well. Bends well with steam. Not durable. Finishes well.
Movement: Moderate.
Uses: Chair rungs and rockers.

Hardwood $$ ▶

Holly

White. Straight, fine grain.

Weight/Strength: .50 sp gr. High strength, fairly stable.
Workability: Difficult to work with hand tools. Accepts glue well, holds fasteners well. Not durable. Sands to great smoothness, finishes very well.
Movement: Moderate.
Uses: White accents on almost any project.

Hardwood $$$ ◗

Ipe*

Light to dark olive-brown. Tightly interlocked grain, fine texture.

Weight/Strength: .85 to .97 sp gr. Strong, stable.
Workability: Hard to work, dulls tools quickly. Accepts glue well, turns well, holds screws well (use pilot holes). Very durable. Finishes well.
Movement: Moderate.
Uses: Flooring, fine tool handles.

Hardwood $$ ●

Lauan-meranti*

Red-brown to pale pink to light yellow. Straight grain, coarse texture, axial resin ducts visible.

Weight/Strength: .34 to .68 sp gr. Moderately strong, reasonably stable.
Workability: Lauans work easily, heavier merantis are more difficult. Accepts glue well, holds fasteners well. High resin or high silica content is hard on blades. Not durable. Fill to finish well.
Movement: Moderate to low.
Uses: Plywood for backing (U.S.).

Hardwood $ ●

Mahogany*

Red-brown. Very straight grain.

Weight/Strength: .39 to .56 sp gr. Medium strength, stable.
Workability: Works easily, though reaction wood may make it difficult to work. Accepts glue well, holds fasteners well. Durable. Finishes well, needs filling.
Movement: Low.
Uses: Fine furniture.

Hardwood $$ ○

Maple, soft

Light-beige heartwood. Straight grain, fine texture.

Weight/Strength: .49 sp gr. Strong, medium stable.
Workability: Accepts glue well, holds fasteners well. Not durable. Finishes to a superb gloss. Some stains may blotch.
Movement: Moderate to high.
Uses: Turning, general woodworking, and furniture.

Hardwood $ ●

Maple, hard

Very light-tan or beige. Straight grain, fine texture. Found in bird's-eye, fiddle-back, and curly figure.

Weight/Strength: .56 sp gr. High strength, stable.
Workability: Works well with all tools. Turns well, accepts glue well, and holds fasteners well. Not durable. Stains readily, finishes nicely.
Movement: Moderate to high.
Uses: Cabinets, furniture.

Hardwood $$ ●

Oak, red

Reddish-brown. Straight, coarse grain.

Weight/Strength: .63 sp gr. Strong, reasonably stable.
Workability: Works well. Accepts glue well, holds fasteners well (drill pilot holes—do not use ferrous fasteners; they cause black stains). Not durable. Stains readily, fill for smoothest finish.
Movement: Moderate to high.
Uses: Furniture, cabinetry.

Hardwood $ to $$ ●

Oak, white

Light tan-brown. Straight grain, ray flecks in quarter-sawn wood.

Weight/Strength: .68 sp gr. Very strong, stable.
Workability: Works with reasonable ease. Accepts glue well, holds fasteners well (with pilot holes). Durable. Stains evenly, takes a smooth finish.
Movement: Moderate.
Uses: Furniture wood—quarter-sawn figure is exceptionally popular.

Hardwood $ to $$ ●

Padauk*

Red-purple-brown with red streaks.
Interlocking, ribbon figure when quarter-sawn.

Weight/Strength: .67 sp gr. Very
strong, stable.
Workability: Works easily. Accepts glue well,
holds fasteners well (use pilot holes). Very
durable. Finishes very well.
Movement: Moderate to low.
Uses: Furniture and cabinetry.

Hardwood $$ ▶

Pine, white*

Light brown, often with red tint. Straight grain.

Weight/Strength: .35 sp gr. Medium strong,
stable once dried.
Workability: Works easily, but deposits resin
that gums up tools. Holds fasteners well.
Not durable. Finishes well.
Movement: High.
Uses: Carving, toys, secondary wood
for furniture.

Softwood $ to $$ ○

Poplar*

Gray-white to gray-brown. Straight grain.

Weight/Strength: .38 sp gr. Medium
strength, stable.
Workability: Works easily. Carves and turns
nicely. Accepts glue well, holds fasteners
well. Not durable. Stains blotch, finishes
well. Use sealers.
Movement: Moderate.
Uses: Secondary furniture, cabinets.

Hardwood $ ●

Selecting & Working Common Woods

Poplar, Yellow (tulip)

Yellowish brown, with streaks of green, purple, black, blue, red. Straight grain.

Weight/Strength: .40 sp gr. Medium strength, stable.
Workability: Works very easily. Accepts glue well, holds fasteners well, does not split easily. Not durable. Seal before staining. Paints well.
Movement: Moderate.
Uses: Secondary furniture wood.

Hardwood $ ●

Purpleheart

Purple after exposure. Straight grain, medium to fine texture.

Weight/Strength: .67 to .91 sp gr. Very strong, stable.
Workability: Works easily with power tools. Accepts glue well, holds fasteners well (use pilot holes). Durable. Finishes well with wax and clear finishes.
Movement: Moderate to low.
Uses: Decorative projects, accents, general cabinetry, tool handles.

Hardwood $$ ●

Rosewood, Indian*

Golden brown to dark purplish brown, with black streaks.

Weight/Strength: .70 sp gr. Strong, stable.
Workability: Hard to work by hand, dulls tools, needs slow cutting. Accepts glue well, holds fasteners well. Durable. Fill before finishing. Takes a high polish.
Movement: Moderately high.
Uses: Tool handles, small decorative objects.

Hardwood $$$ ◗

Sassafras*

Pale brown to orange-brown. Straight grain, coarse texture.

Weight/Strength: .42 sp gr. Not strong, stable.
Workability: Works easily with hand tools. Carves nicely, turns well. Accepts glue well, holds fasteners well (use pilot holes). Durable. Finishes well.
Movement: Moderately low.
Uses: Boxes.

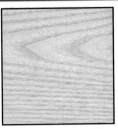

Hardwood $ to $$ ◗

Spanish Cedar*

Light to dark reddish brown. Straight grain, fine texture.

Weight/Strength: .40 sp gr. High strength. Medium stability.
Workability: Easy to work. Accepts glue well, holds fasteners well. Durable. Finishes well.
Movement: Moderate.
Uses: Boxes, furniture, cabinetry.

Hardwood $$ ○

Sycamore

Reddish brown with lighter-colored sapwood. Interlocking, even grain, fine texture, great quarter-sawn figures.

Weight/Strength: .46 sp gr. Medium strength; quarter-sawn is stable, plain-sawn is not.
Workability: Works easily with sharp hand tools, burns if feed is too slow. Not durable. Plainsawn tends to warp and cup. Finishes well, test quarter-sawn with each stain.
Movement: High in plain-sawn, lower in quarter-sawn.
Uses: Cabinetry, furniture.

Hardwood $ to $$ ●

Teak*

Yellow-brown to dark golden-brown. Straight grain, coarse, uneven texture.

Weight/Strength: .55 sp gr. Strong, stable.
Workability: Works easily. Dulls tools quickly. Holds fasteners well, use polyurethane glues for best results. Durable. Requires clean up with mineral spirits or alcohol before finish is applied.
Movement: Moderate.
Uses: Outdoor projects, chairs, benches.

Hardwood $$ ●

Tupelo (black gum)

Light-brown with a gray cast. Fine, uniform texture, interlocking grain.

Weight/Strength: .46 sp gr. High strength, stable.
Workability: Very difficult to turn, carves well. Tends to burn when fed too fast. Accepts glue well, holds fasteners well. Not durable.
Movement: Modest.
Uses: Small projects, cabinetry.

Hardwood $$ ●

Walnut, black*

Purplish brown to grayish brown. Best when air-dried. Even grain, coarse texture. Fiddleback, crotch, and burl figures.

Weight/Strength: .51 sp gr. Strong, stable.
Workability: Works easily. Deep cuts may cause tear-out. Accepts glue well, holds fasteners well, turns well. Durable. Open grain needs filling, finishes well.
Movement: Ratio is 1.4.
Uses: Fine furniture, boxes, cabinets.

Hardwood $$ to $$$ ●

Willow, black*

Gray-brown. Interlocking grain, finely textured.

Hardwood $ ●

Weight/Strength: .36 specific gravity. Low strength, stable.
Workability: Accepts glue well, holds fasteners well. Not durable. Clear finishes work well.
Movement: Low.
Uses: Woven wood baskets.

Bonding Ability of Popular Woods

	U.S. Softwoods	U.S. Hardwoods	Imported Woods
Bond Easily	Eastern White Pine; Western White Pine; Western Red Cedar	Alder; Aspen; Basswood; Cottonwood; Willow, Black	Balsa; Purpleheart
Bond Well	Sugar and Ponderosa Pine; Eastern Red Cedar	Butternut; Elm (Rock); Soft Maple; Sweetgum; Sycamore; Tupelo (Black Gum); Black Walnut; Yellow Poplar	Avodire; Jarrah; Mahogany; Meranti; Spanish Cedar
Bond Satisfactorily	Yellow Cedar; Southern Pines	Ash; Beech, American; Birch; Cherry; Hickory; Hard Maple; Oaks (Red & White)	Bubinga; Meranti (dark red)
Bond with Difficulty	—	Osage Orange; Persimmon	Greenheart; Rosewood; Teak

Woods that bond easily bond with a wide range of adhesives under a variety of bonding conditions.

Woods that bond well may be difficult to bond with some forms of phenol-formaldehyde adhesives.

Woods that bond satisfactorily bond under a fairly wide range of bonding conditions.

Woods that bond with difficulty can often be easily bonded with special adhesives such as the polyurethanes. Please see our adhesives chart, pages 82–85, for further details.

CHAPTER 1

Janka Measurement of Wood Hardness

Wood hardness tells how well a wood does its job in rough use. It also measures how difficult or easy a wood is to work. The Janka test uses a .444" (11.28 mm) diameter steel ball and measures the force it takes to bury that ball half its diameter into the wood. The test is commonly used to check wood for flooring. Higher numbers mean harder woods.

Wood Type	Force Needed
Alder	590
Ash	1320
Balsa	75
Basswood	410
Beech, American	1300
Bloodwood	2900
Bubinga	1980
Cedar, red	506
Cherry	950
Ebony, Brazilian	3692
Goncalo Alves	2160
Hickory/pecan	1820
Jarrah	1910
Lignum vitae	4500
Mahogany, Honduras	800

Wood Type	Force Needed
Maple, hard	1450
Oak, red	1290
Oak, white	1360
Padauk, African	1725
Pine, white	380
Poplar	540
Purpleheart	1860
Rosewood	3170
Teak, Brazilian	3540
Walnut, black	1010
Yellow birch	1260
Yellow pine, longleafa	870
Yellow pine, shortleaf	690
Yellowheart	1820

Possible Reactions to Woods

Wood	Class (Irritant or Sensitizer)	Reaction Type
Alder	Irritant	Respiratory, eye and skin
Ash	Irritant	Respiratory
Avodire	Irritant	Respiratory, eye and skin
Baldcypress	Sensitizer	Respiratory
Beech	Sensitizer	Respiratory
Birch	Sensitizer	Respiratory, nausea
Black locust	Irritant	Nausea
Bubinga	Irritant	Eye and skin
Red cedar, Eastern	Irritant	Respiratory, eye and skin
Red cedar, western	Sensitizer	Respiratory
Cocobolo	Irritant	Respiratory, eye and skin
Ebony	Irritant & sensitizer	Respiratory, eye and skin
Elm	Irritant	Eye and skin
Goncalo alves	Sensitizer	Eye and skin
Greenheart	Sensitizer	Respiratory, eye and skin
Ipe	Irritant	Respiratory, eye and skin
Mahogany	Irritant	Respiratory, eye and skin
Maple (usually only spalted)	Sensitizer	Respiratory
Oak, red	Irritant	Nasal
Padauk	Irritant	Respiratory, eye, skin, and nausea
Purpleheart	Sensitizer	Eye and skin, nausea
Rosewood	Irritant & sensitizer	Respiratory, eye and skin
Sassafras	Sensitizer	Respiratory, nausea, and nasal cancer
Teak	Sensitizer	Eye and skin
Walnut, black	Sensitizer	Eye and skin
Willow	Sensitizer	Nasal cancer

Potency	Source	Incidence
No info	Dust	No info
No info	Dust	No info
No info	Dust	No info
Small	Dust	Rare
Great	Dust	Rare
Great	Dust	Rare
Great	Dust	Rare
No info	Dust	No info
No info	Dust	Common
Great	Dust, leaves & bark	Common
Great	Dust & wood	Common
Great	Dust & wood	Common
Small	Dust	Rare
Small	Dust & wood	Rare
Extreme	Dust & wood	Common
No info	No info	No info
Small	Dust	Rare
Great	Dust	Rare
Great	Dust	Rare
Extreme	Dust & wood	Common
Small	Dust & wood	Rare
Extreme	Dust & wood	Common
Small	Dust & wood	Rare
Extreme	Dust	Common
Great	Leaves & bark	Common
Great	Dust	Common

Defects in Wood

Some wood defects are obvious. Some become obvious later, like internal pin knots, for example.

Wane
Bark along the edge of the board, or missing wood along the edge of the board, usually caused by bark dropping off.

Checking
Splitting of the board, usually at the ends, but also at other spots.

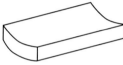

Cupping
Warping across the width of a board.

Warping
Distortion of the wood's shape.

Bow
Warping along the face that runs from one end to the other.

Bend (or Crook)
Warping along the edge that runs from one end to the other.

SELECTING & WORKING COMMON WOODS

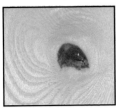

Knots
Parts of branches that the expanding tree has overgrown.

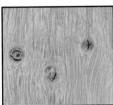

Pin knots
Knots less than ¼" in diameter; spike knots are cut on a long axis.

Encased, or black, knots
Knots that are loose, but remain in the tree.

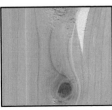

Solid knots
Knots that show no signs of rot or looseness.

Sap stain
A bluish stain caused by fungi in and on wood.

Hardwood Grading

Hardwood lumber uses four basic grades: FAS (for "Firsts and Seconds"), a grade combining the two top qualities; F1F (for "FAS One Face"), FAS on one side but not on the other; Select; and #1 down to #3B Common. Walnut has an additional figure grading standard. Hardwood is supplied in random widths and lengths, and this affects the grade.

When buying, consider the two common grades #1 and #2. Join several narrow common boards edge-to-edge to create wide boards where needed. Edge-joined wide boards tend to be more stable than single-piece wide boards and can be matched for figure to look like one piece.

FAS clear lengths have over 81% of the face clear of defects, on a board width of 6" and a length of from 8' to 16'. FAS boards must be at least 6" wide, and 8' long, and 83⅓% of the board must be clear. The board can only be cut once to yield the percentage needed.

F1F meets FAS standards on one face only, with the second face being a #1 Common.

Select gives 83% clear of defects, but on a board width of 4", lengths from 6' to 16'. Select boards are graded to the same standards as FAS, but with a size of 4" x 6'. The reverse side may be either Select or #1 Common.

Common grades get more complex in cuts allowed.

#1 Common boards are at least 3" wide by 4' long, with 66⅔% of the board clear. Cuts allowed: one-third of the board measure plus one for cuts, with width after each cut to be no less than 4" x 2' or 3" x 3'. A board that is 4 board feet (for example, 6" x 8') is a 4 board measure. One third of 4 +1 is 1. Thus, a single imaginary cut is allowed.

#2 Common must be at least 3" wide by 4' long. Clear yield can be as little as 50%. The surface area after each cut must be 3" x 2'. Anything less than a #2 Common is seldom useful.

To get the best value in hardwood lumber for your project, you'll want to understand the above guidelines, and then use them in a common-sense way. Arrive at the lumberyard with a list of the materials that you need, and keep an open mind in terms of how to fulfill your objective. For instance, if you need to make an 8' x 3' tabletop, then you might be limited to using a premium grade of lumber such as FAS. These boards will probably be straighter, wider, and easier to join together. You'll pay a premium for this kind of lumber. When it comes to building a table base, however, you'll probably mostly need shorter, narrower pieces, so you might want to check out the #1 and #2 common grades. These boards will have more knots or other defects, but if you're clever, you can plan your work and cut around them. Your reward? You'll save as much as fifty percent.

Tip: Always bring a sketchpad to the lumberyard. Lumber varies greatly in terms of dimensions and prices, and you might just stumble across something unexpected that will work out great if you can be flexible and think on your feet.

Buying Softwoods

When it comes to buying softwoods, I usually find I get the best deal at home centers as compared to devoted lumber stores, although your experience may vary. I also have enjoyed visiting a couple of the sawmills outside of town—the hour drive is sometimes worth it just as a fun trip, and I've scored incredible deals this way on the rough-sawn wood that I use for outdoor products. Depending on where you live, you may discover that you have some great resources if you look around a bit.

Softwood lumber grading follows a system similar to hardwood lumber grading, but I don't recommend immersing yourself in it. The problem lies in the fact that a lot of softwood lumber tends to warp and twist even after it has been graded, which means that, practically speaking, the grade designations are often of little value. For example, when I look through lumber at home centers, there are often three grades of pine lumber,

Selecting & Working Common Woods

but the quality varies a lot even within one category. Therefore, I always buy softwood lumber based strictly on appearance rather than being constrained by grade categories that can seem rather arbitrary. With this in mind, I always look at the least expensive stuff first: sometimes I'll get lucky and find what I need there. Other times, I end up having to purchase boards from the more costly section. In any event, selecting softwood lumber isn't much different than hardwood lumber—a common sense approach is your best bet.

Tip: If you don't already know this trick-of-the-trade, you'll appreciate it. To determine how straight a board is, hold it up with one end near your face and the other end angled down toward the ground. You can now look down the entire length of the board and you'll easily get a feel for the board's relative straightness. Some will bow considerably, while others will be straight as an arrow. Generally speaking, you'll probably want to be a stickler and discard those that don't conform to your project specs.

Grading for Cherry and Walnut

Extra allowances in grading are made for cherry and walnut.

Cherry may have an unlimited number of pin knots, no larger than ⅛" in diameter. Gum spots and streaks are also allowed. Red and white oaks may have mineral spots and streaks, to a total of no more than 8⅓% of the cuttings. Poplar is allowed mineral spots and streaking up to 16⅔% of the cuttings.

Walnut grading meets a slightly different standard. It is grouped into 5" wide and wider, 6' long and longer, with minimum sizes of 4" wide by 3' long or 3" wide by 5' long. Five-inch-wide pieces that are 2' to 7' long must yield 83% clear face in two cuttings; five-inch-wide pieces that are 8' and over must yield 83% clear face, but can do so in three cuttings. Pieces 12' and over must yield a 91% clear face.

Walnut figure grading is subjective and not adhered to by all dealers. It is primarily a musical instrument grading system, but it may be used in other situations.

Grade	Appearance
Grade A (1)	Plain, small pin knots.
Grade AA (2)	Clear, free of all knots, may have occasional figure or grain pattern.
Grade AAA (3)	Crotch walnut, marbled grain, lightly flamed straight grain (no crotch)
Grade AAAA (4)	Attractive figure throughout, flame, marbled, crotch.
Grade AAAAA (5)	Highly figured, almost never seen outside musical instruments, veneers.

Plain-Sawn, Quarter-Sawn, and Rift-Sawn Wood

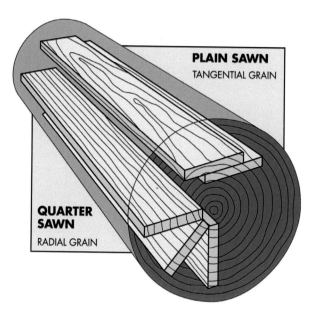

Plain-sawn wood is also called flat-sawn. The log runs through the mill in one piece, and each slice is cut all the way through the log. Plain-sawing produces lumber that is often considered the most attractive. It also conserves the lumber, producing the most usable lumber from any particular board. Spike knots are less likely to occur than with quarter-sawing. Shake and pitch pockets are found in fewer boards. Thickness swelling is less. Most wood is plain-sawn. It requires less skill from the sawyer and is easier to find.

Quarter-sawn logs are cut in quarters first, through the log center. Each quarter is then sawn. Some sawyers flip the cant after each cut, some don't. Results vary because of this. Quarter-sawn lumber is more stable in width, an important quality when building furniture. There is less cup and twist with quarter-sawn stock and fewer surface checks and splits during drying and in use. It wears more evenly. Quarter-sawing also brings out rays, interlocked grain, and ribbon figures more noticeably than plain-sawing. Sapwood in boards appears at the edges. Quarter-sawn lumber does not generate boards as wide as those that are plain-sawn.

Rift-sawn lumber, also called bastard-sawn, is cut from quarters, but the quarters are set at a 15° angle during sawing, producing lumber that has about a 30° to 60° angle to the log, versus the 45° and under of plain-sawn and the 45° to 90° of quarter-sawn. Rift-sawn lumber is a mid-range style. Angles are approximate because of changes in angle as each board is cut.

Surfaced lumber: All green lumber and much seasoned lumber is bought unsurfaced for later jointing and planing. For the novice wood selector, **S2S** is a good start: **S2S** lumber has two sides surfaced. For ready-to-use lumber, look for either **S3S** (surfaced three sides) or **S4S** (surfaced four sides). **Skip planing** gives the buyer a look at parts of the surface, allowing more accurate judgment of wood quality than is possible with totally rough wood.

You may also see these terms: **R1E** is Ripped one edge (may also be called "side"); **R2E** is Ripped two edges; **J1S** and **J2S** indicate boards that have been joined for greater width.

Storing Wood

Storing wood is as important as selecting it. Wood is best stored flat, with enough support to prevent it from warping and sagging. Indoor storage of seasoned wood is best.

Stickers: Remember to square (cross-section) sticks, or stickers, that you use to separate layers of drying lumber. Stickers are usually ¾" x ¾" x the width of the stack. Stickers must be dry no matter how wet the unseasoned stack is. Wet (green) stickers stain the areas where the stickers and drying wood meet. Dry wood does not need to be stickered if the storage space is dry, but it is not hurt by proper stickering either.

Stacks: When outdoors, stacking and stickering lumber is the accepted method of storage, to keep air flowing. Protection of the top layer is necessary; plastic and old sheet metal roofing make good covers. Weight well with cement blocks or rocks.

Drying Lumber

Lumber dries fast in a kiln. Kiln drying speeds up the availability of seasoned wood, often reducing wood-drying time to three-or-four weeks instead of a year or more. Solar kilns are the simplest, and you may find that building your own kiln may be easier than finding a local operator to take small amounts of green wood.

Steaming: For some woods, steaming is done in conjunction with kiln drying to even out the colors of the wood. Walnut is a spectacular example. Its purplish, deep-brown evens out to a duller brown, and the brown moves into the sapwood, which is normally almost white.

Basic Air Drying: For basic air drying, the rule of thumb is one year for each inch of rough, green lumber thickness. In very humid areas, it takes longer, possibly 18 months. In very dry desert areas, wood may be ready in six months. Measure the moisture content with a moisture meter when the stack is finished. Check every six months. You're looking for the wood to reach equilibrium moisture content (EMC, around 12% to 16% in most of the U.S. and Canada).

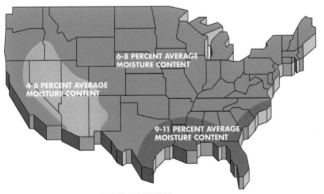

6-8 PERCENT AVERAGE MOISTURE CONTENT

4-6 PERCENT AVERAGE MOISTURE CONTENT

9-11 PERCENT AVERAGE MOISTURE CONTENT

COURTESY HARDWOOD INFORMATION CENTER

Equilibrium Moisture Content: EMC is the point where wood neither accepts nor releases moisture to the surrounding air. It is a changing attribute, depending on the relative humidity of the wood's environment. Passing thunderstorms or two-week-long dry spells mean that the EMC changes, sometimes a great deal and sometimes rapidly. (The lowest used is about 6%. There is always some moisture movement within wood after drying, so actual content may vary a point or two over a month and more from winter to summer). Non-production woodworking is often done with 10% moisture content. Production woodworking needs lower percentages. Expect problems with wood that was used in especially humid climates if it is moved to a desert area, and vice versa.

This moisture meter shows cedar ready to use at 10%.

Moisture Content Change Rates

Moisture Content Change	Approx. Change In Width
1%	1/128"
4%	1/32" scant
8%	1/16" scant
12%	5/64" full
16%	7/64" full
20%	9/64" full
24%	11/64" full

Change rates vary with wood species, finish, and size.

Above is for solid oak in 2¼" width.

Chart information courtesy of Hardwood Manufacturers' Association.

Finish air drying lumber by drying it in the warmest, lowest humidity spot available. This is often the attic. In modern homes, attics consist of trusses that are not meant to be heavily laden. Older homes have rafters and ceiling joists that can take a heavier pile of wood. For truss style roof framing, spread the load carefully. For most of us, it is more practical to use a dry corner of the basement. Use a dehumidifier, if needed, to keep the humidity down. Do not start drying wood in the hottest spot you have. That leads to degradation.

Movement

Wood remains a living material after it is cut, seasoned, and turned into furniture. This defines the characteristic of movement. Care must be taken to see that wood movement doesn't ruin projects.

- Glue up narrow boards to make wide tops and sides so there is less tendency to warp and cup.
- Most wood movement is across the board. Allow for it. Attaching tops to table aprons is done with fasteners or techniques that allow wood to move as its moisture content changes. Mount wide boards, such as tabletops, with oval shaped screw holes, so there is room to move or slot the apron on the inside, and use an "L" fastener that slips into the slot and is screwed to the underside of the table top. Do the same on wide shelves and other parts, or otherwise allow for movement.
- Sliding dovetails work well for shelves that must be fixed without glue (or with just a dollop in the center or to one end of the dovetail). The shelf is still strong enough to help prevent racking forces from twisting the project.
- The sides of inserted panels in doors must be made to float, rather than be glued in solidly.

Always let wood acclimate to shop conditions before starting work. If you don't, the wood will still be acclimating and moving as you machine and assemble needed parts. Usually, a 72-hour acclimation period is sufficient.

Selecting & Working Common Woods

CHAPTER 1

Ordering Lumber

When it is time to order lumber for a project, it pays to do your homework before you go to the lumberyard. You will avoid having to make extra trips to your supplier.

Species: Ask for a specific wood species, not merely a broad family name. For example, order "white oak," not just "oak." Every species has unique properties; select one with the characteristics that suit the needs of your project.

Quantity: Lumber is measured in either linear feet or board feet. Linear foot measurements apply only to material that is sold "by the running foot," and this includes anything that is labeled 1" x 4" or the like. For example, a 6' long 1 x 4 would be measured as 6 linear feet. A 6' long 1 x 10 would also be 6 linear feet. Retailers would then have a different price code for each type of board. Moldings are identified and sold in this same way. A 6' long piece of crown molding, for example, would measure out at 6 linear feet, regardless of its width. To determine the value, the seller would just multiply the per foot cost times six. This system is pretty straightforward; it is mostly applied to softwood lumber, although home centers sometimes use it for hardwoods as well.

SELECTING & WORKING COMMON WOODS

Measuring lumber in board feet is a bit more complicated, but it is necessary for measuring non-uniform lumber that varies in width and thickness. As shown in the diagram, the standard board foot is equivalent to a piece that is 1 inch thick, 12 inches wide and 12 inches long. To calculate the number of board feet in a particular piece of wood, multiply its three dimensions together. Then divide the result by 144 if the dimensions are all in inches or by 12 if one dimension is expressed in feet. For the standard board, the formula is:

1" x 12" x 12" ÷ 144 = 1 (or 1" x 12" x 1' ÷ 12 = 1)

So if you had an 8-foot-long 1-by-3, you would calculate the board feet as follows: 1 x 3 x 8 ÷ 12 = 2 (or 2 board feet). Other examples are shown in the illustration on page 48.

Tip: Even after many of years of experience, selecting the right amount of lumber can still feel like a very abstract process. To simplify the process, I call upon the mental image of an 8 foot long board, 1" thick, and 6" wide. It is easy for me to remember that this is 4 board feet, and I then have that as a rough standard to use as I'm going through a stack of boards. If I need 50 board feet, for example, then I know that I'll need about 12 or 13 boards of that size. If the boards are a bit smaller, I'll need more, and if they're bigger, I'll use fewer. When I think I'm close to 50', I can then measure the whole lot at once (or have a lumberyard employee do it) and add or subtract additional boards as needed to meet my goal.

Size: Wood is sold in nominal rather than real sizes, so remember to make allowances for the difference when ordering surfaced lumber. A 1-by-6 piece of pine, for example, is actually ¾ inch thick and 5½ inches wide when dried and surfaced. With rough, or unsurfaced green lumber, the nominal and real sizes are the same. The thickness of hardwood boards is commonly expressed as a non-reduced fraction in quarters of an inch. A 1-inch-thick oak board, for example, is termed 4/4 lumber, a 1½-inch-thick plank is 6/4 and so on.

Grade: When ordering a particular grade of wood, use standard terminology. The main differences between higher and lower hardwood grades lie in appearance rather than strength. In general, reserve higher-grade wood for the visible parts of your projects.

Seasoning: Lumber is sold either kiln-dried (KD) or air-dried (AD). The practical difference between the two is that KD wood has a lower moisture content, about 8 percent, while air-dried, high-density hardwoods generally have a moisture content range of 20 to 25 percent. Softwoods and lower density hardwoods are air-dried to 15 to 20 percent moisture content. KD lumber is therefore preferable for making indoor furniture, because the wood is unlikely to dry out any further; as well, the kiln's heat allows the wood's cells to reposition, reducing the likelihood of warping and checking. This does not mean you need to restrict yourself to buying only KD lumber, however; in fact, many carvers prefer moister wood, making AD wood a better choice for them.

SELECTING & WORKING COMMON WOODS

Surfacing: Also known as dressing, surfacing refers to how lumber has been prepared at the mill before it is sent to the lumberyard. Lumber that is surfaced is usually surfaced on both sides: S2S lumber has been planed smooth on both faces, while S4S wood has had both faces planed and both edges jointed. Rough, or unsurfaced, lumber (Rgh) is less expensive than either S2S or S4S wood, and if you own a planer and a jointer, you can save money by surfacing rough lumber in your shop.

Flexibility: Make sure to take a look around and see all the options. There are probably more than you realize. Inventories also fluctuate, and many times I've gone in looking for one thing and then seized an unexpected opportunity for something better. Sometimes I'll make spur of the moment design changes simply based on what's available—if I see a stack of unusually pretty cherry, I might abandon my plan of using maple, for example. Similarly, my main lumberyard often has closeout prices on small quantities of lumber that they just want to get rid of, and I'm happy to take advantage of these serendipitous finds. Looking around in this manner is also just a good way to get an education and learn about species you haven't used before.

A sample order for wood at a lumberyard might be as follows: 100 bd. ft. $\frac{8}{4}$ FAS (Firsts and Seconds) red oak, S2S. This would amount to 100 board feet of nominally 2-inch-thick FAS grade red oak with both faces planed smooth.

Number of Board Feet in 4 Linear Feet of Different Size Boards

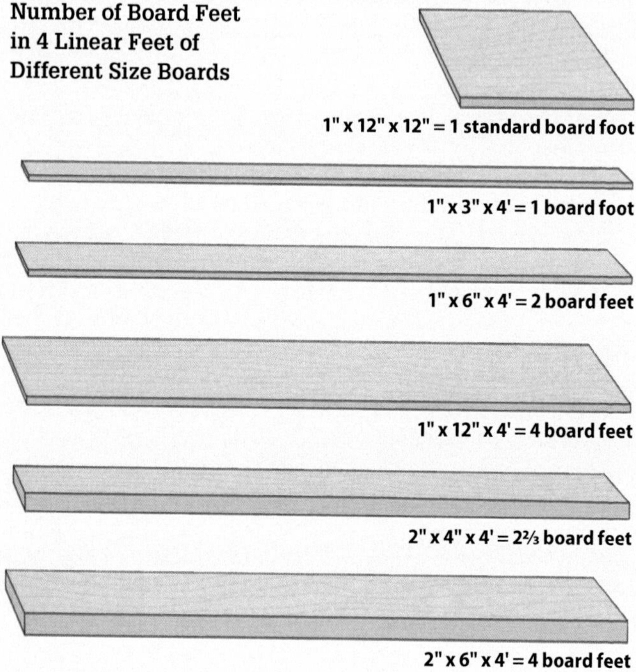

1" x 12" x 12" = 1 standard board foot

1" x 3" x 4' = 1 board foot

1" x 6" x 4' = 2 board feet

1" x 12" x 4' = 4 board feet

2" x 4" x 4' = 2⅔ board feet

2" x 6" x 4' = 4 board feet

Selecting & Working Common Woods

Fasteners: Nails, Screws & More

The world of wood fastening can be fascinating and frustrating. Knowing what's available, and where each type is best used, is very important if you want to stay fascinated while reducing frustration.

CHAPTER 2

Nails

Nails can be an important part of wood joinery, offering an easy way to strengthen joints. They come in a variety of shapes and sizes, corresponding to their intended use.

Commonly Used Nails. Probably the most useful to most woodworkers are finishing nails, casing nails, and brads. **Finishing nails** are slender with a somewhat rounded head, and **casing nails** are slender with an inverted cone-shaped head. Similar to finishing nails, **brad nails** are slender with a rounded head and are relatively short; usually 2d or under in length (1" or less.)

Understanding Nail Sizes. Penny sizing, a practice that goes back to 15th-century England, continues to puzzle many people. Back then, nails were sold for a certain number of pennies per hundred. Today, they're sold by the pound, but the old designations still apply. The charts below and on page 51 show nail penny sizes, their corresponding inch measurements, different head types, and uses.

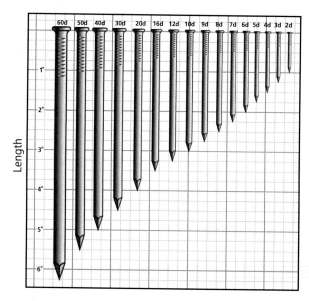

Fasteners: Nails, Screws & More

Chart of Common Nail Sizes and Uses

Penny Size	Length	Diameter	Head Type	Where To Use
2d	1"	.072"	Small	Finish work
2d	1"	.072"	Large, flat	Small wood
3d	1¼"	.08"	Small	Finish
3d	1¼"	.08"	Large, flat	Small wood
4d	1½"	.098"	Small	Finish
4d	1½"	.098"	Large, flat	Small wood
6d	2"	.113"	Small	Finish
6d	2"	.113"	Large, flat	Small wood, slightly larger projects
7d	2¼"	.113"	Small	Finish, casing, stops, etc.
7d	2¼"	.113"	Large, flat	Sheathing, siding, flooring
8d	2½"	.131"	Small	Finish, casing, baseboard, wainscot
8d	2½"	.131"	Large, flat	Sheathing, siding, flooring, framing, general small shop work
9d	2¾"	.131"	Small	Casing, baseboard, crown
9d	2¾"	.131"	Large	Sheathing, siding, subfloor, light framing
10d	3"	.148"	Small	Casing, baseboard, crown
10d	3"	.148"	Large, flat	Sheathing, siding, subfloor, light framing
12d	3¼"	.148"	Large, flat	Sheathing, subfloor, framing
16d	3½"	.162"	Large, flat	Framing
20d	4"	.192"	Large, flat	Framing
30d	4½"	.207"	Large, flat	Heavy framing
40d	5"	.225"	Large, flat	Heavy framing
50d	5½"	.244"	Large, flat	Very heavy framing
60d	6"	.262"	Large, flat	Very heavy framing

Wire Nails vs. Cut Nails. Wire nails, the typical round, machine-made nails, are more commonly used than cut nails. Cut nails differ from wire nails most obviously in shape. The head of a cut nail is rectangular, and the shank has the appearance of a wedge. Many believe that cut nails hold better because of the way the shank pushes the wood aside, after which it springs back and grips. Cut nails are readily available to woodworkers in a variety of types, ranging in size from 1" to 4" in approximately ¼" steps. Penny sizes are not used. These nails can be used to give a period accent to many woodworking projects.

Pneumatic Fasteners

Air-powered tools have become readily available. For most woodworkers, finish nailers, brad nailers, and staplers are exceptionally handy. The latter two are reasonable in price and can be coupled with a low-cost, low-capacity air compressor to do a lot of good work.

Nails for air-powered tools

Lengths of pneumatic-use brads start at about ½" and go to 2". Finishing nails run from 1¼" to 2½". Brads and shorter finishing nails can be substituted for clamping in difficult areas while glue sets and need not be removed.

Staples for air-powered tools

Staples vary more because they come in several head widths. For most woodshop uses, ¼" and ½" widths are all that's necessary. Wide staples hold upholstery well, especially those with fabrics that will tear or fray. Narrower staples have a range of applications and can often be used in place of brads. Note that a different stapler is needed for each different staple head width.

Wood Screws

While nails are generally considered the best fasteners if you don't expect to take a project apart, screws work well for projects you expect to disassemble. They are non-destructive fasteners that can be easily removed. You'll find numerous types of screws available, specifically for use in wood.

Types of Drive. The three most-used drives for woodworkers are slotted, Phillips, and square-drive.

 Slotted screw heads are most often used in reproduction work today.

 Phillips screw heads are used for power driving purposes and are superior to slotted screw heads.

 Square-drive screw heads are used for power driving purposes and are superior to slotted screw heads. This type of screw head is the best so far at preventing cam-out, a factor in scarred surfaces on finished projects.

Types of Screw Heads. The most-used head types are flat, pan, and round; however, the oval and the washer-head (the washer is part of the lower screw head) are also common.

 Flat Head
(abbreviated fl. hd.) Easily countersunk so that the screw sits flush with the surface or sits below the surface to be concealed.

Pan Head
Used to fasten hardware and to strengthen joinery.

 Round Head
(abbreviated rd. hd.) Decorative. Used when the screw cannot be countersunk.

 **Oval Head**
Decorative. Used when the screw cannot be countersunk. Often used with washers.

Washer Head
Used to give greater strength.

Fasteners: Nails, Screws & More

CHAPTER 2

Sizes

Screws need to be sized to the job. The thicker the stock, the longer and thicker the screw needs to be. Most woodworking is done with relatively small wood screws (#4, #6). Heavier projects, including most outdoor projects, take larger wood screws (#8, #10, #12 and #14).

Screw length and shank thickness are related. Small diameter screws seldom come in very long lengths, though some thick screws do come in short lengths. For example, a #3 screw, the next-to-smallest available, comes in lengths only up to ¾". A #12 screw comes in lengths from 1" up to 3", while a #14 goes up to 3½", with the shortest being 1¼".

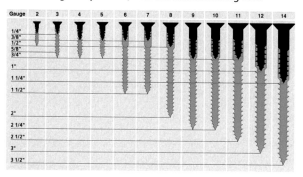

Screw Materials

There is no single best material for a screw; it all depends upon the application.

Hardened steel screws are the workhorse for many situations, but are entirely unsuitable for most exterior applications unless properly coated or plated.

Unplated hardened steel screws are the most popular and are primarily used where they will not be visible or exposed to corrosive conditions. Color, whether pure black, bronze, or silvery gray, does not affect quality. Unplated screws treated with a dry-lube finish reduce driving torque requirements, but this finish does not provide corrosion resistance.

Stainless steel screws are softer than hardened steel screws and are noncorrosive.

Aluminum screws are surprisingly strong because the aluminum hardens as it is formed into screws. Some manufacturers use aircraft grade aluminum for screw manufacturing. These screws work well for assembling aluminum doors, windows, or gutters because they eliminate the corrosion problems that zinc-plated fasteners have.

Solid brass screws are very soft and demand a carefully sized pilot hole to eliminate installation breakage. Pre-threading the hole with a steel screw helps minimize this problem. The softness of the brass greatly increases cam-out problems, a situation neatly overcome by a square drive. Brass screws should not be used when high shear strength is needed.

Silicon bronze screws are primarily used for marine boatbuilding, but many people use them to build decks made of western red cedar or redwood because the screws will eventually blend into the color of the wood. Screws right off the production line are the color of a fresh penny. They eventually oxidize and darken as shown in the picture.

Fasteners: Nails, Screws & More

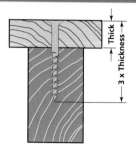

Determining Screw Length

Using the correct length screw is imperative. Always start the screw through the thinner piece, threading it into the thicker piece. It's best to have about ⅔ of the screw length go into the thicker piece. Most wood screws are threaded only ⅔ of the way up from the tip, a quality that should aid you in choosing the proper length. The unthreaded portion should equal the thickness of the thinner piece. Shorter screws, 1" and shorter, are usually threaded all the way. As the pieces get thicker, you can reduce the percentage of screw length going into the heavier piece. Countersink or counterbore to make sure no threaded part remains in the thinner piece. Screws inserted with threads in only the thicker board draw the two pieces tightly together. If threads are in both pieces, they'll never draw up tightly.

Screw Dimensions

I've listed screw dimensions in maximum and minimum decimal dimensions, and in maximum fractional dimensions. Note that the fractional dimensions are the best approximations of the actual decimal dimensions.

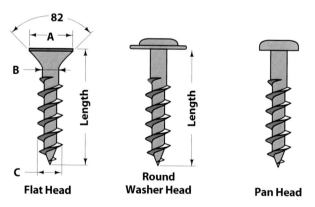

Flat Head

Round Washer Head

Pan Head

Dimensions for Flat, Round Washer, and Pan Head Screws

Screw Head Decimal Dimension

	A – Flat Head		A – Round Washer Head			A – Pan Head		
Size	max	min	max	min	T max	max	min	T max
4	0.225	0.195	0.219	0.205	0.086	N/A	N/A	N/A
6	0.279	0.244	0.270	0.256	0.103	N/A	N/A	N/A
8	0.332	0.292	0.322	0.306	0.120	0.376	0.352	0.110
10	0.385	0.340	0.373	0.357	0.137	0.443	0.411	0.125
12	0.438	0.389	0.425	0.407	0.153	N/A	N/A	N/A
14	0.507	0.452	0.492	0.473	0.175	N/A	N/A	N/A

Body and Thread Dimensions

	B – Body Dia	
Size	max	min
4	0.095	0.084
6	0.118	0.107
8	0.136	0.125
10	0.157	0.146
12	0.176	0.165
14	0.201	0.190

	C – Thread Dia	
Size	max	min
4	0.116	0.105
6	0.142	0.131
8	0.168	0.157
10	0.194	0.183
12	0.220	0.209
14	0.246	0.235

Note: IFI Standards specify a tolerance on screw length of +0", -1/16".

Head, Body, and Thread Fractional Dimensions

	A – Flat Head	A – Pan Head		A – Round Washer Head		B – Body Dia	C – Thread Dia
Size	Max Dia	Max Dia	T max	Max Dia	T max	Max	Max
4	7/32	7/32	3/32	NA	NA	3/32	1/8
6	9/32	17/64	7/64	NA	NA	1/8	9/64
8	21/64	21/64	1/8	3/8	7/64	9/64	11/64
10	25/64	3/8	9/64	7/16	1/8	5/32	3/16
12	7/16	27/64	5/32	N/A	N/A	11/64	7/32
14	1/2	31/64	11/64	N/A	N/A	13/64	1/4

Fasteners: Nails, Screws & More

CHAPTER 2

Selecting Bits for Pilot Holes

Drilling pilot holes for your screws helps to eliminate problems, such as installation breakage and cam-out.

Drill Bit Shapes. To select the appropriate bit, start by checking your screws. If the screw has a straight shank, use a straight drill bit to poke the pilot holes. If the sides of the screw taper to their points, then use a tapered drill bit.

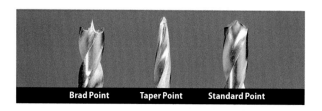

Brad Point   Taper Point   Standard Point

Drill Bit Sizes. Pilot holes should match the diameter of the screw shank inside the threads, so the threads cut clean pathways and give the most strength. Use a slightly larger bit for hardwoods and a slightly smaller one for softwoods. Make sure that the hole depth matches the screw penetration into the second piece of wood. Otherwise, the screw may not develop full holding power. The tables on pages 59–60 provide good starting points.

Tips for Using Soft Metal Screws. If you are using softer metal screws in hardwoods, such as brass screws in oak, you'll want to use a same-size steel screw in addition to drilling a pilot hole. Drill the pilot hole, then run a same size steel screw with wax-lubricated threads into the pilot hole. Remove the steel screw and drive the softer brass screw. This method greatly reduces the number of wrenched-off heads on brass screws.

Tips for Using Square Drive Screws. Drilling a pilot hole with a straight drill bit yields excellent results because the screw shank is straight throughout its entire length, except for the point. The reduced shank diameter at the head means an enlarged body hole isn't necessary. The straight bit also doesn't require the critical depth control needed with a tapered bit.

Pilot Hole Diameters for Wood Screws

Hardwood			
Screw Size	Drill Bit Size (fraction, inches)	Drill Bit Size (decimal)	Drill Bit Size (number)
#0 & #1	³⁄₆₄	0.047	58, 55
#2 & #3	¹⁄₁₆	0.063	53, 51
#4 & #5	⁵⁄₆₄	0.078	48, 44
#6 & #7	³⁄₃₂	0.094	42, 38
#8	⁷⁄₆₄	0.109	35
#9 & #10 & #11	⅛	0.125	32, 30, 29
#12	⁹⁄₆₄	0.141	27
#14	⁵⁄₃₂	0.156	20
#16 & #18	³⁄₁₆	0.188	16, 10
#20	⁷⁄₃₂	0.219	3
#24	¼	0.250	D

Softwood			
Screw Size	Drill Bit Size (fraction, inches)	Drill Bit Size (decimal)	Drill Bit Size (number)
#0 & #1	¹⁄₃₂	0.031	69, 65
#2 & #4 & #3	³⁄₆₄	0.047	59, 56, 55
#5 & #6 & #7	¹⁄₁₆	0.063	53, 52, 50
#8 & #9	⁵⁄₆₄	0.078	48, 46
#10 & #11 & #12	³⁄₃₂	0.094	44, 43, 39
#14	⁷⁄₆₄	0.109	34
#16	⅛	0.125	31
#18	⁹⁄₆₄	0.141	29
#20	⁵⁄₃₂	0.156	26
#24	¹¹⁄₆₄	0.172	18

Countersink Diameter (82°)		
Screw Size	Countersink Diameter (Fractions, inch)	Countersink Diameter (Decimal, inch)
#0	1/8	0.125
#1, #2	3/16	0.188
#3, #4, #5	1/4	0.250
#6, #7, #8, #9	3/8	0.375
#10, #11, #12, #14	1/2	0.500
#16, #18	5/8	0.625
#20, #24	3/4	0.750

Fasteners: Nails, Screws & More

Square Bit Tip Sizes

Bit Tip Dimensions			
Bit Size	Max	Min	Fraction
#0	0.071	0.0696	1/16+
#1	0.091	0.090	3/32-
#2	0.1126	0.111	7/64+
#3	0.133	0.1315	1/8+
#4	0.191	0.1895	3/16+

Confirmat Style Screws

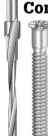

This specialized screw is designed to allow easy and sturdy screw assembly of MDF. They are almost essential in the assembly of cabinets made of melamine-coated MDF. The shoulder is designed to lock the shank in position, while the shank is extra long to reduce chances of pull-out. These screws require a pilot hole through both pieces of material. The pilot hole must be produced with the correct screw drill bit if it is to work properly.

CHAPTER 2

Pocket-hole joinery has been around, in one form or another, for thousands of years. The technology was made accessible to woodworkers around the world almost 30 years ago when the Kreg Jig™ was introduced. It consists of a simple jig that drills a pilot hole and a larger hole at a 15 degree angle so that nearly any two pieces of wood can be joined in a number of different ways. The technique is simple yet effective, and it allows even novice woodworkers to join wooden components without the need for complicated math or esoteric joinery. It should be in every woodworker's toolkit.

Another useful and versatile modern system that many woodworkers enjoy is biscuit joinery. The oval-shaped, pressed-wood biscuits are available in a few different sizes, and they fit neatly into slots that are cut by a dedicated machine called a biscuit joiner. After cutting a half-slot in two different pieces of wood, the slots are then filled with glue, and the biscuit is inserted into the slots. The two pieces of stock can then be clamped together. The moisture in the glue causes the biscuits to expand to form a virtually unbreakable joint. Biscuits can be used to join boards together edge-to-edge to create a tabletop, and they can also be used at various other angles so that pieces can be joined in many other ways, too.

Dowel joinery is similar to biscuit joinery, but it involves larger intermediary pieces. A pair of large dowels—say ⅜" in diameter—can create a very strong right angle joint that may even be suitable for fine furniture. Most dowel jigs are quite inexpensive—around $20–40—and the good ones are self-centering and can accommodate dowels of different sizes.

Loose tenons are not loose, except as compared to standard tenons. A special tenon stock is used, or made, and a jig is used to drill a series of holes to make a mortise that will fit the tenon. The tenon is then fitted, as shown, into those drilled out holes, with glue, and the second piece is fitted. This is a quicker procedure than cutting a tenon with a saw, and cutting out a mortise with a chisel or a mortising machine.

Fasteners: Nails, Screws & More

Designing for Movement

Wood moves significantly in width and barely at all in length. Designing for movement is vital in cross grain joints, such as frame-and-panel doors or tabletop-to-apron joints. Failure to do so may result in some very unpleasant experiences, such as split panels. It's best to force wood to move in the desired direction by establishing a fixed reference point. Then, slot fastener holes at other attachment points to allow for movement.

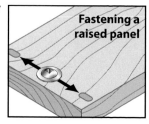
Fastening a raised panel

- **Raised panels** are pinned in the middle of their width, so movement takes place equally to either side.
- **Table tops** may be similarly fastened, but if they are fastened as shown at right, the entire width absorbs the movement, allowing an overhanging edge to disguise the movement.

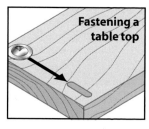
Fastening a table top

- **Table-top-to-apron attachments** need commercial steel Z, figure 8 hardware, or shop-built blocks and Z shapes. Always allow for top movement, which may be as much as ½" (across the grain) in large solid wood tables. Whenever tabletops are wide (over about 8"), make sure to allow for wood movement.

Wood Movement and Moisture

Wood movement is proportional to moisture change, so a complete moisture barrier on all wood surfaces is important. Varnish and polyurethane prevent many seasonal moisture changes and minimize the effects. A 1% moisture change would result in ⅙ the movement predicted by the chart below.

1% Moisture Change		
	Flat-Sawn:	Quarter-Sawn:
Hardwoods	¼" per 12"	⅛" per 12"
Softwoods	5⁄32" per 12"	3⁄32" per 12"

Fasteners: Nails, Screws & More

Inserts

Brass inserts provide great strength and allow for easy and frequent assembly and disassembly. They work in jigs, among other projects.

Brass Threaded Insert Sizes:
8–32; 10–24; ¼–20; $\frac{5}{16}$–18; $\frac{3}{8}$–16.

Stainless Steel Threaded Insert Sizes:
8–32; 10–24; ¼–20.

Using the Insert. Thread the insert into a properly sized hole, and use machine screws to do the actual holding. The hole you need is the same diameter as the body of the insert. Screwdrivers may work in soft woods with inserts; insert drivers are a better option in harder woods. Start with a bolt the same size as the insert threads, cut the bolt head off, and run two nuts down until they jam together. Place the double washers under the two nuts (between the bottom nut and the top of the insert). Run the insert in with a power drill. The insert driver for manual use (socket or open-end wrenches) is even simpler: Use double washers under the bolt, and leave the head intact.

Tips: Use stainless steel threaded inserts for exterior projects. For hardwoods, stick with the larger insert sizes. The small threads on the smallest two sizes (#8–32 and #10–24) do not work well in hardwoods.

T-Nuts

T-nuts are for exterior use and also provide great strength. They are useful in jigs and exceptionally handy in making adjustable leg levelers and similar devices. The hole is drilled, and the T-nut is driven in. The sharpened tangs around the perimeter of the upper part drive into the wood and hold very well.

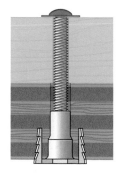

Other Fastening Devices

Included here is a list of other types of fasteners that can be useful in woodworking.

Machine Screws

Machine screws come in a variety of sizes, but usually are found in only two head types: round-head and flat-head. They work particularly well with brass inserts. Brass machine screws should be used with brass inserts to prevent metal-to-metal corrosion. Stainless steel inserts are also available. The wood screw size chart on page 54 should provide general guidelines for machine screw sizes.

Carriage Bolts and Lag Screws

These fasteners work well for holding heavy loads against wood objects or holding heavy wood objects against other materials.

Carriage bolts offer no-spin necks that crush the wood as they enter, creating a head that doesn't turn and a smooth surface that doesn't catch. Several neck styles are available.

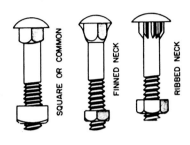

SQUARE OR COMMON   FINNED NECK   RIBBED NECK

Lag screws are important in many situations. They are especially useful in situations where there is no access to the rear side, something that's needed with square-head and carriage bolts. Lag screws come in square and hex-head versions.

Metal Screws

Less useful than woodworking screws (in wood projects), metal screws are still an essential ingredient to woodworking success in many situations. Basic types work well for most projects. There are quite literally hundreds of other types to fit special needs.

Fasteners: Nails, Screws & More

Washers and other additions to security

Washers under the heads of lag screws and bolts reduce or eliminate the destruction of wood fibers when the nut is cranked down tight. In extreme cases, use washers under both the head and the nut. Note that carriage bolts do not accept washers under their heads. Other washers are used to keep vibration from eventually loosening nuts.

FLAT WASHER   SPLIT LOCK WASHER   SHAKE PROOF WASHER

The drawing above shows common types of washers. There are other types for special situations; however, the ones shown here are the ones most-used by woodworkers.

Metal brackets and braces

Here are a few types of braces, in brass and steel. Their utility is great, but their use often suggests a sign of a lack of joint-making skill.

- T-braces work to secure pieces that form a "T" with each other.
- Corner braces can be placed inside any two pieces that form a right angle, and there are three-way types available that can be placed inside three pieces.
- Straight braces are available and are sometimes useful for spanning two board ends.
- Metal stanchions with cut-outs to fit shelf support clips can make for faster adjustable shelf installation. Simply rout two grooves in each side, nail or screw in the stanchions, and add clips for the shelves.
- Adjustable shelf brackets rest in holes drilled in the sides of the cabinet. These brackets support shelves very well.

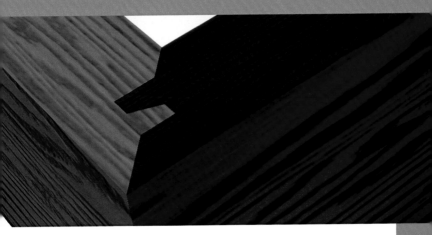

CHAPTER 3

Guide to Woodworking Joints

Joints are the foundation of almost all woodworking. Tight, solid joinery provides the basis for attractive and long-lasting projects. Woodworkers are constantly developing new joint variations, so providing a complete listing is impossible. But you'll get the basics you need right here.

Guide to Woodworking Joints

Wood Joints from Weakest To Strongest

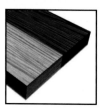

Butt Joint

A butt joint is made by joining two pieces of wood together edge to edge, side to side, or end to end. Edge joining boards produces wide wood stock that doesn't move as much as wide boards. Shear strength is low; the wide surface is generally supported at the ends, the back, the front, or the sides. Splines and biscuits can be used with butt joints to add strength and to create a better alignment.

Uses: Making wide boards from narrow boards.

End-Grain-to-End-Grain Joints

As the name suggests, an end-grain-to-end-grain joint is made by joining two pieces of wood end to end. These joints are among the most difficult to make strong, but modern adhesives work remarkably well. Several different profiles add strength and tighten alignment.

Uses: Making longer boards from shorter boards.

Dowel Joints

Dowel joints are typically butt joints that use dowels to strengthen the joint. Aligning dowels is tricky, and woodworkers have developed many jigs and aids to help. The simplest aids—dowel centers—work quite well. Dowels are easy to place in almost any shape, as long as you can match surfaces and dowel holes. Small dowels work well in light stock, which is not always the case with other joint supports.

Uses: Chair rungs, door frame strengthening. Often used with butt and miter joints to help add strength and to ease alignment.

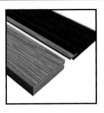

Spline Joints

Spline joints are made by cutting slots into the two boards you wish to join and fitting a separate piece of wood, sized so that the boards touch, into the slots. Splines are used to add strength to butt joints and to ease alignment woes during glue-up.

Uses: Often used with butt and miter joints to help add strength and to ease alignment.

Biscuit Joints

Biscuit joints use a system of slots and football-shaped plates of pressed birch to help align a joint, make glue-ups easier, and add strength. It is a type of spline joinery made easier by a single purpose machine.

Uses: Often used with butt and miter joints to help add strength and to ease alignment.

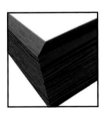

Miter Joints

Miter joints are butt joints cut at an angle. This type of joint may be reinforced with splines or biscuits to increase strength. Miter joints are used extensively in door casings, cabinet trim, and similar spots. One form of joining decorative trim that uses a mitering technique is called coping a joint. One side of the joint is mitered, while the other is butted against the object. (This only works with inside joints.) The mitered joint is then coped—with a coping saw—to fit the butted section.

Uses: Frames (door and picture), boxes.

Guide to Woodworking Joints

Lock Miter Joints

Lock miters are miter joints in which each board has a slot and a groove that fits into its mating board's slot and groove. These joints are made with lock miter router bits. A word of caution: be sure to use the bits in a router table, never freehand.

Uses: Boxes, drawers.

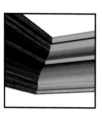

Compound Miter Joints

These joints include two angles—one lengthwise and one normal miter angle. Compound miter joints are useful when shapes are more complex, as in projects with sloping sides. Most long bevels can be done with a taper jig to give the correct slope.

Uses: Joining crown molding at outside and inside room corners.

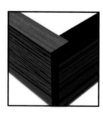

Rabbet Joints

A rabbet is a ledge cut onto a board, into which another board is fitted, as in the back of a bookcase. Rabbet joints are basically stress-free.

Uses: Inserting backs in constructs (bookcases, shelves).

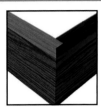

Miter and Rabbet Joints

The miter joint and rabbet joint are sometimes combined to make a useful corner lock-type joint for drawers and other box corners. Today, this lock joint is most often made with a specific type of router bit, but it may also be made with a table saw.

Uses: Drawers, boxes.

Dado Joints

A dado joint is made by cutting a slot (dado) in one piece of wood, and then fitting another piece of wood into the dado. Dado joints are considered housed joints—joints that are enclosed on at least one side.

There several different types of dado joints, the most common of which are:

- Through dado joints: the inserted board is visible on both outside edges of the outside board. (The illustration above is a through dado joint.)
- Stopped dado joints: one side of the dado (or both, if desired) stops short of the edge of the outside board, answering one of the objections to dados—their edge appearance.
- Rabbeted dado joints: a ledge is cut into the inserted board and fit into its corresponding slot.

Dados are cut by hand, with a table saw, and with a router. For most cabinetmaking purposes, dados are limited to ½ the thickness of the wood that is being dadoed or grooved. If the wood is very thin (½" or thinner), dados should be ⅓ the depth and will need some form of support under the dado's bottom edge.

Uses: Shelves, bookcases, etc.

CHAPTER 3

Lap Joints

Lap joints are made by cutting grooves in two boards and fitting them together at the grooves. These joints are easy to design and construct—they are easily cut by hand or by machine. Though it's a common misperception that all lap joints are half-laps, this is not the case.

To make a **half-lap joint**, cut away half the thickness of each piece and fit them together, so that the two overlap. Half-laps are popular and resist stresses in several directions. They may be done at corners, in the middle, or in other interior parts of the boards. Corner half-laps are actually matching rabbets.

Dovetail lap joints are decorative and useful, with more racking strength from the wings of the dove's tail than is available with a straight half-lap.

Uses: Egg-crate-type assemblies (half-laps), projects requiring separators.

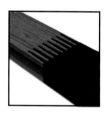

Box (Finger) Joints

Box joints are made up of alternating tenons and grooves on each of the boards that will be fit together. They are one of the strongest joints for producing rectangular structures. There are probably hundreds of uses for these versatile and easy-to-make joints. Simple jigs make production fast and easy on table saws and router tables. They may also be cut by hand, which can be time consuming and difficult, or with power tools, which is fast and easy. Joint variants are many, including vertical doweling down through the fingers for strength, rounding or chamfering the edge, or setting loose with a dowel insert as a pin and the fingers forming a hinge.

Uses: Boxes, drawers.

Dovetail Joints

Similar to the box joint, a dovetail joint is also made up of alternating tenons and grooves; however, these tenons start narrow and become wider, giving them a dovetail shape. Dovetail joints provide exceptional strength in the types of stresses that drawers receive, but they are more difficult to make neatly than other joints. Commercially made jigs for producing dovetails abound. With a good dovetail saw with rip teeth and a set of decent chisels, dovetails can be done by hand with relative ease. Once the process is mastered, hand cut through and half-blind dovetails become a sign of quality and are useful for jobs that require fewer than a dozen drawers.

Uses: Drawers, cabinet carcasses, shelf carcasses, shelves, boxes.

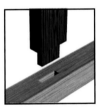

Mortise-and-Tenon Joints

A mortise-and-tenon joint is made by cutting a groove (mortise) in one board and cutting a tab or projection (tenon) in the mating board. The tenon is then inserted into the mortise to fit the boards together. Often used in barns and houses in the past, mortise-and-tenon joints are becoming popular once again. These joints are useful in many types of framing, including cabinetry, doors, drawer fronts, and windows.

One of the most popular machines on the woodworking market today is the benchtop mortiser, specifically designed for this type of joint.

Handcutting a mortise is easy, though getting neat mortises is harder. Tenons are easily formed with a saw, either a handsaw or a power saw of almost any type, with the bandsaw being the easiest to use.

Tips for sizing: One-half the width of the member being mortised is available for the tenon.

Uses: Frames (cabinet doors, building doors, buildings, barns, homes).

Guide to Woodworking Joints

CHAPTER 3

Variations on the mortise-and-tenon joint
Bored and pinned mortise-and-tenon joints, shown at left, have pins to give extra support, are easily made with hand tools, and give exceptional strength.

Haunched mortise-and-tenon joints, which have an extra shoulder (haunch) and corresponding notch, resist racking forces better than straight joints. Use this type of joint in wood more than 4" or 5" in length or when wood strength appears weak.

Stub mortise-and-tenons lay out almost the same way as through mortise-and-tenon joints, but, because the tenon does not go all the way through its mating board, you must mark the depth.

Open mortise-and-tenon joints are similar to bridle joints, in that the mortise is cut only partway through the wood and the tenon is visible.

Tongue-and-groove joints are a weaker form of mortise-and-tenon.

Wedged and foxed mortise-and-tenon joints are both wedged, but **simple wedged mortise-and tenon joints** are through mortise-and-tenons, with wedges inserted into the tenon end or through the top of an exposed part of the tenon. **Foxed mortise-and-tenon joints** are blind mortise-and-tenons, with the mortise splayed a bit to accept the spread of the tenon as the tenon is pushed, and the wedges move into the tenon to spread its end. Depending on project size, wedges extend about ¼" to ½" from the tenon or more on larger joints.

Bridle joints are a form of mortise-and-tenon joints. The drawing here shows its slight difference from the open mortise-and-tenon: the bridle joint can be used in the length of a board.

Figuring Miter and Bevel Angles

If you are working with an object with vertical sides, it's easy to find the angles needed to form a polygon. Start with the number of sides. Divide 180° by that number. Subtract the result from 90°. Thus, the equation for an equilateral triangle would be 180 divided by 3=60. 90-60=30°. For five sides, divide 180° by 5 to get 36. 90-36=54. For eight sides, 180 divided by 8=22½. 90-22½=67½.

Guide to Woodworking Joints

Clamps

The first job anyone has when getting ready to buy more clamps, especially if the clamps aren't needed for an immediate job, is to figure out how the new tools will be used, where they will be used, and how often they'll be used. Once these things are determined, it's fairly easy to select the proper clamp for your needs.

Always be careful not to over-crank your clamping jobs. Few glues demand high clamping pressures—resorcinol is one, though it is typically used in boatbuilding. A properly fitted joint eliminates any need for extreme pressure with most glues. If the joint doesn't fit well, it's often better to redo the joint than to increase the clamping pressure. Polyurethane glues offer many of the same properties as resorcinol adhesives. Polyurethane adhesives take a moderately high clamping pressure, but the joint can still be glue-starved if too much pressure is applied.

Pipe Clamps. The pipe clamp is basically a flat panel clamp. Sizes accept ½"- and ¾"-diameter black iron pipe, threaded on at least one end. Accessories are clamp pads and saddles to hold the clamps off the benchtop. Pipe clamps change lengths easily. Clamp fixtures mounted on 5' pipe can be changed to longer or shorter pipe to suit the job at hand. Length is unlimited, though the bending strength of ¾" black iron pipe limits use to something under 16'. Black iron pipe is preferred because the clamp adjusters slip on galvanized pipe. Because black iron rusts and picks up grime and grit, use waxed paper between the pipe and the wood being clamped to keep the pipe from staining the wood.

Bar Clamps. In some instances, lightweight, aluminum bar clamps are more appropriate for a project than pipe clamps. Aluminum bar clamps are lighter than equivalent length pipe clamps and may be easier to use. However, these lightweight clamps can't apply as much pressure as pipe clamps. Steel bar clamps allow great pressure, even more than pipe clamps. The positive clamping action is similar to aluminum bar clamps.

Corner Clamps. Corner clamps come in many sizes and are most often used for cabinet face framing, assembling carcass panels, assembling cabinet stiles and rails for doors, and assembling bookcase verticals to horizontals. Lightweight picture framers' clamps usually work, but the need for heavier stock in two different sizes at the joint often requires a heavier clamp. Picture frame clamps provide a gap that allows a trim cut on the corner stock.

Cam Clamps. Cam clamps are quick-action, light-duty, and light-pressure bar clamps that are ideal for instrument making. Guitar makers use many of these. They are available in sizes up to and past 30", and some come with deep throats for larger work. Many have cork or other soft facing materials on the pressure faces. The lever that activates the cam provides only light pressure.

C-Clamps. C-clamps provide very strong pressure in a confined area. When working with C-clamps, be sure to place a scrap piece of wood between the work and the clamping surface to protect the work and to help spread the pressure. The best of the edge clamp designs is an adaptation of the C-clamp with a center post and a pressure point that screws into place after the dual posts are screwed down on a panel surface. This way, the edging is tightly clamped in place. C-clamps are cost effective and useful when many small clamps are needed.

Hand Screws. Hand screws are one of the most underused clamps. The wooden jaws and steel threads allow for different angles to be set when you are working with non-parallel surfaces and objects. Sizes from 4" to 14" are common today, but these clamps are available in sizes up to 24". Size the jaws by rotating the handles; use the front screw for initial sizing, then apply the final pressure with the rear screw. Keep the jaws clean and free of glue drippings by slipping a bit of masking tape over each jaw.

Guide to Woodworking Joints

Band Clamps. For round, octagonal, or odd shapes, use the band clamp. For light-to-moderate duty, use 1" wide bands. For heavy-duty and wide utility, bands 2" and wider are best. Bands are made of heavy nylon or canvas. Heavy-duty clamps apply as much as 2800 pounds per square inch. Lighter duty bands are about 10' long; heavier duty bands may be twice that long.

Veneer Presses. A veneer press is a screw thread press designed for laminating veneer. Two heavy platens (flat panels) are mounted on either side of the veneer and its base (the item the veneer or laminate is being glued to.) The platens are pressed together by hand screws (with wing nut tops) mounted on a jig that allows the screws to be individually tightened across the platen.

One-Handed Clamps. One-handed clamps are always popular. Being able to adjust and clamp with one hand, while holding an assembly with the other, is a great advantage in many instances. These one-handed, or quick, clamps also work well as general-use bar clamps.

Spring Clamps. Spring clamps are for light clamping duties. They are useful in many applications where relatively light pressure is needed, such as joining long strips of wood and holding items in position for light woodworking operations.

Adhesives

Using glues isn't complex: follow the manufacturer's directions. If you cannot find the manufacturer's directions, use the chart on pages 82–85. The chart provides a great overview of the many kinds of adhesives that are available, but if it leaves you feeling confused, rest assured: most woodworking joints simply call for yellow wood glue. An exception to this is the use of polyurethane glue to join oily tropical hardwoods.

Brands Available. The brands listed on the chart are widely available and are among the most commonly used. Others are available and may serve equally well.

General Uses. The uses listed on the chart are meant to guide you as you are selecting an adhesive; they are not intended to be all inclusive. Read the manufacturer's directions for a full list.

Temperature Sensitivity. Adhesives are temperature sensitive. Some are less sensitive than others, but using them outside the manufacturer's recommended range is a sure step on the road to joint failure. Work to keep the wood and surrounding air within the recommended range of temperatures. Chalking is often a sign that your shop and your wood aren't at the correct temperature.

Heat Resistance and Sandability. A heat resistant wood adhesive or glue is easier to sand and uses less sandpaper in large runs. Low heat resistance adhesive gums up sandpaper long before the abrasive is worn out.

Water Resistance. An adhesive with low water resistance allows a project to be taken apart easily if necessary.

Bonding Time. A glue that takes longer to bond should be used if the assembly is complex and takes longer to put together, so that adjustments are easier. Quick-bonding glues are handy for simpler projects and for projects where an instant hold is needed.

Gap-Filling Properties. Only epoxies have true gap filling properties. It's better to construct a tight joint than to use gap-filling glues.

Creep Resistance. Creep is movement of the glue after it has set. This is useful in some cases, allowing flex in a joint so that it doesn't crack. If a joint needs full rigidity, creep is not helpful. Veneers and laminates need some creep allowance, while chair rungs seldom do.

Woodworking Adhesives Chart

Glue Type	Brands Available	General Uses	App. Temp. Range	Water Resistance	Sandabili
Hot Hide Glue	Lee Valley, Behlen's.	Veneers, carcass assemblies, not for use in humid areas.	140° to 212°.	Very low.	Excellen little sandpap gummin
Liquid Hide Glue	Franklin Chemical, Veritas (fish glue).	The same as hot hide glue, indoors, restoration projects, furniture repair.	70° to 90°	Very low.	Little or r problem with gummin
White Glue	Elmer's.	Useful general purpose, non-toxic glue.	60° and up.	Low.	Low hea resistanc gums sandpape
PVA Yellow Wood Glue	Lee Valley Cabinet-maker's Glue, Titebond, Elmer's Carpenter's Glue, ProBond.	Probably the most used woodworking adhesive on the market. Assembly, other general woodworking uses.	60° but closer to 70° tends to be better.	Modest humidity resistance.	Good hea resistanc sands without gummin
PVA II (cross linked polymer) Wood Glue	Titebond II.	Good for above the water-line high moisture conditions, as in outdoor furniture. Not for total submersion.	Use between 60° and 85°.	Very high water resistance, almost waterproof.	Good hea resistanc low gummin during sanding
Extended Open Time PVA	Titebond Extend, Titebond Extend II.	For the longer assembly times needed for more complicated projects.	65° and 85°.	Water resistant (Type II).	Good hea resistanc low gummin

nding Time	Gap Filling Properties	Creep Resistance	Glue Line Color	Other Qualities
minute open ne, overnight clamping is best.	Poor.	High.	Pale-tan.	Comes in pearls or flakes. Clamps are essential. More easily used with proper heating pots to maintain temperature. Finicky, but does a wonderful job. Works well with veneer presses. Tack time is very rapid, assembly must be pre-planned carefully.
ninutes open, 60 minutes clamping.	Poor.	High.	Pale tan.	Less finicky than hot hide glue, requires no glue pot, is easier to use.
ninutes open, 60 minutes mping time.	Poor.	Moderate.	Translucent.	Not finicky. Not as strong as some other adhesives. Harder to sand cleanly. Low cost. Readily available.
ninutes open, 45 minutes mping time.	Has some gap filling properties.	Low.	Clear to pale tan. Darker colors made for woods such as walnut.	Stronger than white glue. Very easy to use. Low cost. Readily available in many sizes.
ninutes open, 60 minutes minimum) lamp time.	Slight.	High.	Pale tan.	Slightly more costly than standard PVA adhesives. Readily available.
5 minutes open, 45 minutes mping time.	Slight.	Moderate.	Pale tan.	More costly than standard PVAs, but can save money on more complex assemblies. Available in regular and water-resistant varieties.

Guide to Woodworking Joints

Woodworking Adhesives Chart, continued

Glue Type	Brands Available	General Uses	App. Temp. Range	Water Resistance
Polyure-thane	Gorilla Glue, Excel, Titebond.	For joints where moisture may be a problem, for joints where it is difficult to coat both sides of joint with adhesive, for joints where temperatures are low.	50°.	Waterproof in but marine us
Epoxy	Industrial Formulators, West System, System 3, others.	Bonds dissimilar materials (i.e., metal or stone inserts), bonds oily woods (i.e., teak, rosewood). Good for boatbuilding or projects in marine or harsh outdoor environments.	40°.	Waterproof.
Hot Melt	Hotstik, Titebond, others in craft stores.	Temporary adhesives used to hold parts together temporarily. Similar uses to spray adhesives. Also used with small area veneers, in sheet form, applied with a regular iron.	235° and up at gun tip or surface of glue.	Fair.
Cyano-acrylates	Varied, Hot Stuff, USA Gold, Special T, Super T.	Useful for inlays and small repairs. Turners find it handy for coating spalted wood.	50°.	Good.
Contact Cements	Franklin, UGL, Roo Adhesives.	For installing laminates on countertops, other areas.	65°.	Fair.
Spray Adhesive	3M 77, Elmer's Craft Bond.	Useful for holding patterns and lighter templates in place temporarily (often for cutting). Works to hold sanding disks in place.	65°.	Not applicabl
Urea Plastic Resin	DAP.	Excellent general woodworking glue, in powder form.	70°.	Highly wate resistant.

Sandability	Bonding Time	Gap Filling Properties	Creep Resistance	Glue Line Color	Other Qualities
Sands well, much excess can be removed with a sharp knife or chisel before sanding.	20 minutes open, 4 hour clamping time.	Poor, though it gives the appearance of filling gaps.	Moderate.	Brown.	Difficult to store, air moisture can cure adhesive in container. More costly than PVA glues. Sometimes needs misting if wood is very dry. Works well on oily woods. Not attractive with light colored woods.
Most formulas sand well.	Highly variable, depends on ratio of catalyst to resin.	Specially formulated types fill gaps completely.	High.	Clear. May be colored.	Needs care in mixing and handling. Hard to clean up, contains hazardous chemicals. Use respirator, gloves, and goggles. High cost.
Poor heat resistance, gums up sandpaper badly.	30 to 60 seconds, no clamping needed.	Good, but weak.	Not applicable.	Creamy tan.	Doesn't work with heat sensitive materials (few plastics). Can burn skin almost instantly. High cost.
Sands well.	Under 60 seconds in most formulas.	Specially formulated types fill gaps.	Not applicable.	Clear.	Very strong. Comes in thick and thin and medium. Fumes may be irritating to eyes. Instant bond may be a problem when bonded to skin. High cost.
Not applicable.	10 to 60 minutes open, instant adhesion.	N/A	Not applicable.	Not visible.	No clamping needed. Roo products are useful for difficult to install laminates such as melamine, will glue melamine to melamine. Some types can be hard on lungs.
Not applicable.	60 seconds.	Very low.	Not applicable.	Not applicable.	Makes a permanent bond if both surfaces are coated and allowed to dry before pressure is applied, much like contact cement. Readily available.
Sands well.	Clamp overnight.	Moderate.	Moderate.	Tan to amber.	Easy to store in powder form. Unlikely to lose strength in powder form. May cause eye irriation. Moderate cost. Not readily available.

Guide to Woodworking Joints

CHAPTER 3

Tips for Gluing and Clamping

Keeping Clamps Glue-Free

Place wraps of masking tape on the inside tips of your handscrew clamps. The tape keeps glue off the tips and is easily removed and replaced.

Reducing Glue Thickening

As wood glues age, they thicken. Reduce thickening by placing the glue container in a double boiler filled with water and heating it mildly. You can use water to thin yellow woodworking glues, but don't thin them more than 5%.

Glue that is stored in partially full large containers may age faster than glue stored in small containers. There is more surface area for evaporation in larger containers. Keep the container full by dropping enough clean marbles in to raise the level of the glue. The marbles are reusable.

Lengthening Pipe Clamps

Lengthening pipe clamps does not take a new piece of pipe. Buy some connectors and use them to join pipe you already have on hand. Any plumbing supply or hardware store has connectors.

Clamp for Round or Odd-Shaped Stock

A cotton clothesline makes a good clamp for round or odd-shaped stock. Wrap with the line around the project, loop the line around a stick, turn until tight, and then put one end of the stick under the line so it can't unwind.

Get Rid of Glue Quickly

Using a wet rag or paper towel, wipe off glue squeeze-out immediately when working with yellow glue. If it has a chance to harden, it must be sanded off, which requires a lot more time and effort to remove. This is in contrast to the residue from polyurethane glues, which foam up and should be allowed to dry. The excess can be scraped right off when dry.

CHAPTER 4

Hand Tools

Woodworking started with hand tools. Today, many woodworkers use power tools, but all woodworkers use hand measuring and marking tools. Some tasks are more easily and effectively accomplished by hand, and many woodworkers prefer to do as much as possible with hand tools.

CHAPTER 4

Measuring tools

Folding rules are used when measuring inside sizes.

Straight rules from 6" to 72" or longer are used for outside measurements.

Tape measures are used for both outside and inside measurements. The hook on the end of the tape moves to allow for its own thickness. Because tape measures curls inward, tilt the tool so that the edge is closer to the work being measured for greater accuracy.

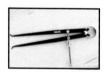

T-squares are rules with a crosspiece mounted perpendicular to the rule, creating a "T." These tools are useful for measuring and marking lines that are at right angles to edges.

Calipers come in inside and outside types. Use inside calipers to measure the interior dimensions of hollow forms, such as bowls. Use outside calipers to measure the wall thickness of bowls or the spacing of reeds in a turning.

Vernier calipers work for inside and outside measurements. Many Vernier calipers have a depth-measuring rod on one end. For most woodworking, a simple type works well. The newest models ease the view by using digital readouts so the user doesn't have to squint his or her eyes to see tiny lines.

Depth gauges are used to measure depths of mortises.

Marking tools

Pencils are useful for marking measurements that don't require a perfect fit.

Awls work well for marking fine lines and for making starting holes for screws and nails.

Marking knives scratch fine lines in wood. They are also useful for scoring and slicing cardboard and paper.

Chalk lines are excellent for marking long, straight lines. The chalk-covered line is drawn taut over the surface to be marked and is snapped to transfer the chalk.

Laser levels offer a greater chance, at a rational price, for woodworkers to align their creations in just a few minutes, without needing to place a level several times.

Hand Tools

Layout Tools

Marking gauges have a wooden arm, a wooden body, and a sharpened pin at one end. The body is set away from the pin at the distance to be marked. The tool is drawn across the surface, with the body firmly pressed against the edge. A marking gauge with two pins is a mortise gauge. Some marking gauges are made of metal, usually a steel arm and a brass body, and use a sharp-edged wheel to cut the line.

Compasses draw arcs and circles and can step out exact distances down a board. Compass scribes transfer markings from irregular surfaces so that flat items can be trimmed to fit.

For larger circles, a set of **trammel points** and a yardstick make a compass that can mark up to 6' in diameter. Trammel points may be attached to longer wood beams for larger circles.

Arches do a wonderful job for large arcs. Cut a 1" x ⅛" thick strip of ash and use a couple of clamps.

Squares

Squares are the most important layout tool. Accuracy and durability are of great importance. Choose a square with a satin finish and etched and filled markings for easy reading.

To check a square, use a straight piece of wood and place the head of the square against the wood. Draw a line along the blade, flip the square's head, and mark again. If the two lines are parallel, the square is square.

Combination squares measure, set router bits for depth, and find squares. For marking, first set the distance on the blade and lock the head. Place a pencil/awl at the end and draw the square and pencil/awl across the object to be marked. Wear and tear can affect accuracy.

Machinist's combination squares with protractor and center finding heads are useful in machine set-up. English measurements are typically broken down into $\frac{1}{64}$", $\frac{1}{32}$", $\frac{1}{16}$" increments. Metric measurements are in millimeters.

Engineer's squares are used for machinery set up. They come singly or in sets, have no markings, and are single purpose: checking for square. The base is thick in comparison to the blade, so the square easily stands on edge.

Sliding T-bevels transfer angles. The angles may be set from a protractor or from the angle to be matched.

Try squares (pictured at the back) check the accuracy of a right angle.

Handsaws

There once were many good handsaws available for all the specific woodworking and carpentry chores. There are fewer today.

European Pattern Saws. Starting a cut with a European saw is simple. Mark the wood. Place the saw on the wood at a 45-degree angle, with the thumb knuckle of the hand not on the saw resting gently against the saw blade. Pull the saw gently to you to score the wood; then push forward to start the cut. As soon as you start taking full strokes, lift the thumb. Use as much of the full blade length as possible without binding and bending when cutting. If the saw binds in the cut, wooden shims keep the kerf open.

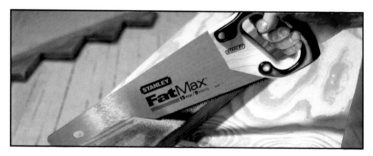

Crosscut saws cut across the grain, with 8 to 12 teeth per inch. The more TPI (teeth per inch), the smoother the cut (the slower the cutting speed). Today's saws are typically 8 or 9 TPI and have hardened teeth that can't be sharpened.

Rip saws have teeth with a chisel shape and usually yield a coarser cut than results from crosscut saws. Dovetail saws are included in this grouping. They are usually from 5 to 7 TPI; dovetail saws have many more teeth per inch. When buying dovetail saws, make sure the teeth are set in a rip pattern. Most of a dovetail cut, as short as it is, is with the grain, so rip teeth work better.

Coping saws cut tight curves in thin stock or molding. Blades can be rotated in the frame to allow cutting in any direction. The fret saw is a taller version of the coping saw, useful for making fret holes in musical instrument tops. The marquetry blade is a very fine-toothed fret saw or coping saw blade.

Bow saws make straight or curved cuts like band saws. The blade is rotated in the frame so that cuts can be made in any direction and in almost any thickness of wood.

Backsaws have a reinforcing ridge across the top back, so the blade does not flex in use. The backsaw is used with a miter box. Dovetail saws and gent's saws are also categorized as backsaws.

Other specialty saws exist—the **veneer saw** is a good example, with a curved blade and tiny teeth designed to cut thin veneer without ruining it.

Japanese Saws. These saws are exceptionally sharp, are pulled instead of pushed, and are easy to control. Dozuki, or Japanese dovetail saws, are easy to use. Because Japanese saws cut on the pull stroke, there is less blade deflection, so the blades are much thinner and have more teeth, resulting in a very thin kerf. Cutting is also fast.

Hand Tools

Chisels

Chisels are more about their sharpening than their actual materials. The best materials with a good edge are preferable; however, a chisel, not necessarily of the best materials, that feels comfortable in your hand and that has a good edge can do a serviceable job. Chisels divide into socket and tang types. The socket chisel has the handle fitted into a socket in the top of the metal chisel; the tang chisel has a lengthy metal tang as a part of the blade that extends into the handle. Generally, tang chisels are not struck with mallets, while socket chisels are.

Bevel-edge chisels include the paring chisel, a tool generally used only with the hand.

Paring chisels take light cuts and are not driven by a mallet. Use one hand to push the paring chisel while you control it with the other hand.

Butt chisels are used with a mallet. They are easy to differentiate from paring chisels—the paring chisel has a longer, slender blade; the butt chisel has a shorter and thicker blade.

Skew chisels are often bevel-edged, but they may also be made for cleaning mortises, in which case they come without bevels. They often come in pairs and are used for cleaning the bottoms of cuts in tight areas.

Cranked neck chisels are used for cleaning out the bottoms of flat grooves (dados).

Mallets supplant hammers in driving sculpting tools and most chisels. Because mallet heads are made of softer material than steel hammers, they do less damage to sensitive handle ends, creating less mushrooming of the end. Mushrooming still occurs; it just takes much longer. Mallet heads are made of copper, brass, leather, wood, and other softer materials, which also makes some mallets handy for driving parts together, or apart, without marring the parts.

Mortise chisels have unbeveled edges, with thick, tapering blades. These chisels are for chopping mortises and are heavy, solidly made tools. Because they chop out and pry out chunks, heaviness is necessary. If you get only one mortise chisel, select one that's ¼" wide. You'll be able to cut mortises ⅓ the width of ¾" thick stock.

Woodcarving

Regardless of the type of tool or technique used, woodcarving is an increasingly popular form of woodworking that provides many hours of enjoyment in making the project and many more hours of enjoyment as people look it over when it's finished. There are several varieties of woodcarving: chip carving, relief carving, Scandinavian flat-plane carving, and whittling, to name a few. Woodcarving tools cover a wide range of shapes and styles; it all starts with the carving knife, which is the entry tool for many wood carvers. From there, the novice may move to gouges, tools with a curved cutting edge used to cut rounds and hollows. Chisels have flat surfaces, either straight or skewed, and are usually used for cleaning up flat surfaces.

Power Woodcarving

Power woodcarving tends to require less physical effort and can be faster, but is just as expressive in modestly different ways. Beginners will use Dremel's small tools, but may then migrate to tools with more power and greater utility. The array of inserts for these rotary tools is astounding.

Woodcarver's Vise

This portable vise, produced by Sjöbergs, can hold relief carvings and smaller in-the-round pieces. If you attach a sacrificial base to the carving, it can be used to clamp almost anything.

Hand Tools

Carver's Chisels

Carving tools often include intricate shapes because some designs are so small that it isn't practical to use a large bladed tool. Needs vary widely, depending on the carver. Some plastic-handled tools have readily removable blades and come in kits that

allow the carver to use one handle with many blade shapes. To get the most out of your carving tools, use them as sharp as you can get them. Look for good quality, and buy the best you can afford.

Parts of a Carver's Chisel

- **Handle:** made of wood or plastic
- **Sharp steel blade:** in one of many shapes
- **Tang:** a shanked-down part of the blade that is fitted in the handle
- **Ferrule:** sometimes fitted to the top of the handle to limit damage when struck with a mallet
- **Bolster:** shaped section between the blade proper and the tang; extra width prevents the tang from jamming into the handle
- **Bevel:** brings steel thickness down to a cutting edge
- **Heel:** where the bevel meets the full thickness of the blade

Carver's Chisel Blade Shapes. Carving tool blades come in two general shapes: flat chisel or curved in cross-section (gouges).

- A **flat chisel** has two bevels, and each side looks the same.
- A **gouge** has a concave surface and a convex one. The concave side is known as the inside or channel of the gouge. The convex surface is the outside or back.

Hand Planes

Hand planes today serve a peripheral purpose for many woodworkers. They smooth board faces, joint board edges, cut rabbets, make moldings, work with or across the grain, and cut dados. When a planer isn't large enough to do the full face of a board, a skilled hand plane user can do that job quickly. There are many types; I've listed common ones here.

Choosing a Plane

Generally, you'll want to consider good fit, good finish, sturdy design, and top materials when choosing a plane.

- **Fit:** Be sure that the shape of the sole matches the shape of the iron. If you have a straight iron, the sole must also be straight; if the iron is convex, then the sole must be convex, and so on. The tote, or rear handle, must fit the hand well. A poor fit on a handle raises blisters.
- **Finish:** The sole itself needs to be highly finished, whether iron or wood, and must be nearly flat. Lignum vitae and iron wood plane soles need to be flattened less often than beech.
- **Design:** The knob, or front handle, is either a horn shape or a ball shape. Look for a plane with a small mouth, which lessens possibility of tear-out. The toe, the edge just in front of the front of the blade, may be the type that can be moved back and forth, so that you can adjust the mouth relative to the thickness of the shaving you want. For jointing or smoothing long boards, use a long plane so it stays out of the dips and gives you a truly flat, smooth surface. A double iron helps cut down on blade chatter.
- **Materials:** Most planes are wood- or metal-bodied. Metal planes now dominate the market, but there are good wood-bodied planes around, some from larger makers and some from individuals. Wooden planes are lighter, but they can warp. Metal planes are heavier, but the extra weight helps to reduce chatter. Cast iron rusts.

CHAPTER 4

Bench Planes

Bench planes are beveled on the bottom edge and are used to smooth stock. The family includes smooth, jack, fore, and jointer types.

Smooth planes are the smallest of the family, ranging from 5½" to 10" long. The smoother is used to smooth smaller surfaces and to clean up around and in spots where the bigger planes don't fit.

Jack planes are 14" or 15" long. The 14" jack plane is classed as a "jack of all trades" plane, able to smooth small surfaces and to clean and smooth larger surfaces.

Fore planes are identical to, but shorter than, jointer planes. Fore planes tend to run between 18" and 20" long. These planes clean up larger surfaces.

Jointer planes are longer than fore planes, starting at 22" and going to 24". These planes clean up larger surfaces.

More Planes

Block planes are short planes, usually with low angle irons, used to cut end grain. They are beveled on the top edge. No top iron is needed because there are no long shavings to break up when cutting end grain. Block plane irons are often set at 20 or 21 degrees; some special block planes have irons set at 12 degrees. For softer woods, 21 or 20 degrees works fine on end grain. The even lower angle of 12° is for harder woods.

Hand Tools

Combination planes were an intended replacement for plow and dado planes. They cut to ¾" deep and have spurs for cross-grain work that are retractable for along the grain work.

Scrub planes are sometimes classed as bench planes. Their bodies are 9½" to 10½" long, and the irons will be 1¼" or 1½" wide. The iron is usually thick. The surface that results will appear gouged and be rounded. Scrub planes work well for the first step in sizing a piece of wood or in removing problem spots.

The **scraping plane** is designed to eliminate most of the need for scrapers. One adjustment bows the blade/iron; the plane does a wonderful job of cleaning up and providing a final surface on many woods. It's especially handy on highly figured woods.

Router planes do what powered routers do today, with much less set-up time. Many of these can cut rabbets, dadoes, stop dadoes, or any other grooves. Some models come with three irons, adjustable by screw.

Rabbet planes come in almost as many varieties as bench planes. These planes clean up rabbets, both bottom and sides and, in some cases, clean the bottoms of dadoes. Rabbet planes are for finish cutting when a table saw or router gives less than perfect results. The irons are usually flush with the sides of the plane body on both sides. There may also be a spur extending out in front of the iron, flush with the plane's side. The spur cuts the wood fibers before the blade gets there, smoothing the way for the heavier-duty cutter in end grain.

Hand Tools

Plow planes are groovers. They're designed to cut a groove of a specific width or larger. Such grooves are used to hold drawer bottoms in place or to hold panels in frames. Most plow planes come with irons of several widths, starting from a narrow ⅛" and going up past ½". A fence maintains the groove's distance from an edge.

A **dado plane** looks similar to a rabbeting plane. Spurs are on the outside edges of the plane, ahead of the plane iron. Most dado planes have depth stops and skewed irons. The sole is usually narrower than the plane's body.

Matched planes are tongue-and-groove planes. One plane is designed to cut a groove, while the other cuts a tongue. They're usually sold in matched pairs so that the tongue will fit the groove.

Miter planes are the ideal tool for creeping up on a perfect miter joint. The frame miter plane is used on small items such as picture frames, while the case miter plane is used on end grain boards, even plywood. The edge miter plane works with the grain on longer boards in casework or coopering. Most of the time, miter planes are used with shooting boards to maintain an accurate edge.

Shoulder planes are a form of rabbet plane, used to clean up tenons in mortise-and-tenon joinery. Sometimes they're used to cut the tenon to size. The plane may have its iron set back into the body or set at the front in a bullnose.

Chisel planes have no sole in front of the iron. They are hard to control, but they work for getting into tight spots, removing dried glue, and trimming plugs.

Screwdrivers

Screwdrivers are among the simplest tools a woodworker has. They are essential for assembling and adjusting, adding hardware, and many other jobs. Today's screwdrivers have ergonomically designed handles, like the ones shown, making them easier and more comfortable to use.

Head Styles and Sizes. Today, screwdrivers come in more head styles and sizes than ever. Less emphasis is now placed on the traditional blade style for slotted head screws. The Phillips head has become the most popular, but it is quickly being supplanted by the square socket screw. Because most screws today are power driven, the head that resists cam-out of the driver tip is likely to become the most popular. See page 53 for different styles of screw heads.

Ratcheting screwdrivers are today's replacement for the nearly two-foot-long Stanley spiral-ratcheting screwdriver that I grew up using. They are lighter, easier to use and cart around, and do a great job of running screws in without tiring the wrist and forearm.

Cordless screwdrivers are a real boon in dealing with assemblies: the various versions tend toward compact heads. All come with a slip chuck that is pulled forward to install or remove a bit, which is a procedure that takes a couple of seconds, allowing quick replacement of a worn bit or quick installation of a different bit style or length. Bit lengths range from 1" to 6".

By using **impact screwdrivers**, it is easily possible to reduce time for installations by many minutes. The photo shows a project built some time ago, with under a minute taken to impact drive four screws.

Tip: It is wise to drill pilot holes to prevent splitting. This is also needed even with hand-driven screws.

Tip: Using square (Robertson) or Phillips drive screws, both readily available in almost all sizes, eases the work of keeping the screwdriver tip in place. It's not a good idea to use slotted screws with power drivers, as the bit tip slips and can mar the work piece.

Drills

The variety of hand drills, and the bits that fit them, is plentiful, though they are not nearly as numerous as they were 25 to 50 years ago. Push drills and egg-beater-style drills are also needed in today's woodworking world.

Types of Bits. Drill bits today are vastly improved. Metallurgy has evolved, and the bits are better. Woodworkers primarily want three types of drill bits. (Spade and auger bits are a fourth possibility.)

Twist bits are essential whenever you're drilling metal and serve well for much wood drilling.

Brad point bits give cleaner holes for dowels.

Forstner bits give flat-bottomed holes, work on slanted surfaces, and will make overlapping holes.

Spade bits do a fast and rough job; auger bits are as fast and produce a cleaner hole.

Drill Bit Materials. Drill bit coatings reduce friction in abrasive materials. Cobalt and titanium are preferred coating materials. Titanium is the cheapest. Cobalt is handy for drilling stainless steel; otherwise it is not needed in the woodshop. Carbide tips are also available.

Hand Tools

CHAPTER 4

Sharpening Drill and Router Bits

Top-quality bits have a lot of engineering behind them.

- **Twist drill bits:** There are jigs available for sharpening twist drill bits on a grinder. With some practice, you can also sharpen a twist drill bit on a grinder without the jig.
- **Spade bits:** Use an auger bit file and maintain factory angles. Lap the tip on both sides to sharpen it.
- **Auger bits:** The tip should not need work; use an auger bit file to file the insides of the flats. File the cutting lip with an upward stroke (toward the shaft of the bit).
- **Brad point bits:** Use an auger bit file to sharpen the brad point bit, filing the chipping bevels.
- **Forstner bits:** Maintain factory angles and use a small round stone to hone the inside rim of a Forstner bit. A slipstone touches up the flat back of chipping bevels, and a fine file does the top angle of the bevel.
- **Router bits:** Use a diamond file and touch up only the flat faces. Maintain factory angles.

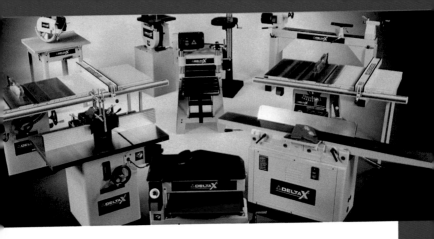

CHAPTER 5

Power Tools

Though hand tools can do most of the jobs that power tools perform, power tools often accomplish the task more easily and with greater speed. When you are selecting power tools for your shop, it is important to consider what power tools will best suit your needs and what space you have available.

PORTABLE TOOLS

Drills

CORDED DRILLS

Corded drills offer amounts of power that cordless tools may never be able to match. One-hand, keyless chucks are now common on all but the most powerful corded drills. For use as a hammer drill, corded surpasses cordless at least up to 36 volts. I would still buy one of the newest dedicated drivers. They are much better, generally, at sensing when to stop driving.

Features to Consider
- **Angled head**—for work inside cabinets and in other tight places.
- **Clutched models**—for driving screws, eliminating the need for buying a dedicated power screwdriver.

CORDLESS DRILLS

Cordless drills, and many other cordless tools, have become mainstays of most woodworking shops. Though not as powerful as corded drills, cordless drills offer the convenience of not needing a power outlet. Most woodworking drilling not taken care of by a drill press falls into a category that does not require a huge, sustained power supply.

Cordless Tool Power
Typically, 18 volts is the common ground, with more powerful hand tool units ranging up to 36 volts for those who need the muscle. For most woodworkers, 18 lithium ion volts is more than sufficient, even when the power pack is driving a circular saw, jig saw, or other heavy duty tool. Lithium ion technology offers great runtime, an immense number of charges (the major sign of a battery's lifetime), and low temperature during the charge cycles.

Cordless Nailers

Some projects require the use of nails, and a cordless nailer is a very effective tool for getting the job done quickly and easily. A few companies make them. Some are battery powered, while others rely on small, inexpensive gas cartridges to drive the nails. Most can fire nails up to 2" long, and they have several advantages over traditional air-powered nailers.

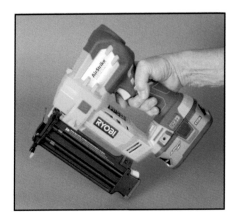

Some cordless nailers use a rechargeable battery that fires a fuel. Paslode makes 18 volt cordless nailguns for brads, finishing nails, and framing and roofing nails. Ryobi makes 18 volt brad nailers and a small finish stapler.

Pros

- Less expensive than the cost of a compressor and nailgun
- Nearly maintenance free
- Portability: no hoses or cords means that you can take the nailer anyplace you'd like
- Convenience: no lost set-up time on job sites or waiting for a compressor to charge

Cons

- A more limited selection of nails to choose from; this is generally not a problem, however.

Multipurpose Tools

Dremel

The Dremel rotary tool line had its inception in 1932 when Albert Dremel introduced a razor blade sharpener. The sharpener forced a reduction in the price of razor blades, thus killing its own market, but Dremel came up with the Moto-Tool, a do-everything small tool, to replace it. Today's much more sophisticated designs are children of that original Depression Era tool. The Dremel tool line accepts an immense number of bits, cutters, and other accessories. It has become a go-to tool for sharpening, small drilling, small sawing, sanding, and almost anything else that can be done with a rotary tool. The newer lithium ion cordless models make it useful literally everywhere.

RotoZip

RotoZip is something of the big brother of handheld motorized tools. It was originally intended as an easy way for carpenters, electricians, and plumbers to make cut-outs in various types of wall materials more easily. It is now used in many other applications and, like the Dremel, offers a cordless model as well as several corded versions, and a host of accessories in the form of dust collectors, blades, drill bits, hole saws, and grinders.

Circular Saws

Circular saws for the woodworker and DIYer are handheld tools that speed the cutting of various wood products, from framing lumber in a wide range of thicknesses to sheet goods such as plywood and medium density fiberboard (MDF).

Generally, saw blades for circular saws are carbide tipped for long life, though steel blades are readily available.

Saw capacities are described by blade diameter: the most popular is 7¼". Blade diameters for corded saws range from 5½" to 16⁵⁄₁₆". The big saw is for beams and timbers: it cuts beams over 6" thick. It weighs more than 32 pounds, compared to 8 pounds or so for a 7¼" saw; 6½", 8¼" and 10¼" saws are readily available.

Cordless circular saws are generally smaller than corded models: Makita offers a 7¼", with a 36 volt battery. Their 12 volt saw has a 3⅜" blade for trim and sheet goods. Milwaukee presents 6½" cordless saws, with corded saws mostly 7¼", though their panel saw uses an 8¼" circular saw.

DeWalt, Hitachi, Porter-Cable, and others carry 7¼", and there are a few 8¼" corded circular saws. Most 18 volt cordless saws stop at 6½"; Ryobi's model is 5½", light and easy to use.

Usually, it's best to select the saw, cordless or corded, that cuts to the thickness one expects to be the greatest in normal use. Cuts to 45° should be checked if buying smaller than a 6½" saw. Any circular saw needs to cut to full depth at the diagonal on a standard 2x4. Saw amperage is an indication of motor strength. In 6½" and up saws, make sure to get at least a 9 ampere corded saw, or an 18 volt lithium ion battery. Skil's worm drive saw draws 15 amps, as do many of the other pro-level saws. Ridgid's 6½" corded saw draws 9 amperes. Any pro-level saw should outlast its owner. Lower-cost saws often expire early and lack power for heavy or continuous work.

The worm-gear-driven SKIL MAG 77LT is today's top-of-the-line version of the original SKILSAW. It is 4 pounds lighter than older versions because of the use of magnesium today. Worm gear saws are powerful and exceptionally durable.

Blade brakes make it safer to sit a saw down, though they don't make up for a lack of sense if the saw's lower guard doesn't release properly. The brakes also speed blade stops for changing blades. Note: When changing saw blades, always unplug the power source, whether it's a cord or a battery.

Power Tools

CHAPTER 5

Scroll Saws

Scroll saws are great tools for beginning woodworkers because there's no chance of kickback, and the danger of losing a finger or two is reduced by the small size of the blades used.

Throat Depth
If you are looking for a scroll saw, be sure to consider the depth of the throat. Many offer a 15" cutting depth, but some go to 24" and more.

Space Requirements
Space needs for scroll saws are small, and portability is great. Even the heavy-duty models can be picked up and carted several feet by one strong person. Most scroll saw work is small, but you need space to move around the saw to get the most effective angles to handle intricate cuts. Count on 3' on three sides.

Power Tools

Jigsaws

Jigsaws are powerful and capable of cutting a straight line (up and down) when needed. Many brands come in two styles—one with a barrel grip and one with a top handle. Most jigsaws can cut wood up to 2¾" thick.

Features to Consider

- **Variable speed**—allows adjustment of speed to cut a variety of stock
- **Orbital blade mechanism**—creates a circular blade movement that changes the aggressiveness of the cuts
- **Tilting base**—allows beveled cuts
- **Tool-free blade changing system**—allows quick blade changes
- **Scrolling feature**—allows the blade to move while the saw continues in a direction, helps to create curved, smooth cuts

Power Tools

Biscuit Joiners

A biscuit joiner quickly cuts slots that are correctly sized for accepting a biscuit. This type of joint replaces most dowel joinery; it may also be used to replace many mortise-and-tenon joints. Consider one with a reasonably sophisticated and easily set fence—the fence improves chances of producing good work at all angles. A rack-and-pinion height adjustment is best. Separate locks for angle and height are easier to use.

Sanders

Power sanders can make quick work of almost any sanding job. There are numerous sanders on the market: large, stationary sanders and portable hand sanders.

There are three kinds of hand sanders: belt sanders, palm sanders, and random orbit sanders. They're all essential equipment in any serious shop, as they function somewhat differently and are best suited to certain tasks.

Belt sanders are great for removing material quickly, especially with a coarse grit belt. You can even find 36 grit belts for fast stock removal. They're also good for flattening high spots on large panels. You'll need to keep the sander moving at all times to ensure that it doesn't wear away one spot too much.

Palm sanders (also called ¼ sheet sanders) are mostly used for finish sanding with high grit (150 and finer) papers.

Random orbit sanders should be your first choice if you can only afford to purchase one sander, as they're the most versatile. They can be used to remove a lot of material at once, and also for finish sanding. Most sanders use a hook and loop (Velcro) system to attach the discs. Discs are available from 36 grit on up. You can also purchase 1000–3000g discs to polish lacquer finishes.

Space Requirements for Stationary Sanders

There are so many different kinds of sanders used in workshops today that describing space needs for all of them is impossible.

- **For a 6" by 48" belt sander**— Give 3' to each side of the disc, plus 4' behind the machine, and 4' leading into the belt.
- **General spacing rule**—Allow at least 3' to stand and move around in, plus enough space for the work pieces.

Power Tools

CHAPTER 5

STATIONARY TOOLS

Table Saws

The table saw is the basic stationary woodworking power tool in most shops. It is capable of making almost every type of cut, even dadoes. As an alternative to the table saw, some woodworkers will use a radial-arm saw or a band saw. The selection of a table saw depends on its intended use. For hobby use, a 10" blade, 1½ hp tilting arbor table saw is the most popular and arguably the most useful.

Types of Table Saws

There are generally four types of table saws: cabinet, hybrid, contractor's, and benchtop.

Cabinet Table Saw: This type is typically the heaviest, most powerful, and largest saw. A cabinet encloses the base of the saw.

Hybrid Table Saw: Hybrid table saws fall between contractor's saws and cabinet saws. They are more costly by a little than contractor's saws, but cheaper than cabinet saws, while offering two important cabinet saw features: the trunnions mount to the cabinet so they are adjustable without turning the saw upside down; second, the cabinets are enclosed, to make attaching dust collection easy.

Contractor's Table Saw: The contractor's saw is not quite as powerful as the cabinet saw; however, its light weight makes it mobile—a benefit in a smaller shop. Many have the motors tightly enclosed, with formed plastic shields at the bottom fitted for dust collection hook-up.

Benchtop Table Saw: Though it is the least powerful of the four, the benchtop saw is powerful enough to perform most woodworking tasks. This type's small size and light weight make it the most portable of the four saws.

Horsepower

For most shops, 1½ to 3 hp is sufficient. For contractor's and benchtop saws, the minimum is 1½; with cabinet saws, you should usually start at 3 hp. Cabinet saws are available in models up to 5 hp without going to three-phase electricity. (Three-phase electricity is industrial quality power.) If power feed is to be used with thick hardwoods, 5 hp is necessary.

Table Size

Contractor's and cabinet table saws will have a table of at least 27" x 36". Rails and fences add more area, as do sliding tables. Some table saws have tables up to 28" x 40" without extensions. Benchtop saws tend to have smaller tables to ensure portability.

Blade Capacity

The blade capacity helps to determine the saw's cutting capacity. A 10"-diameter blade with a 3 hp motor should allow you to cut most woods.

Space Requirements

Spacing around a table saw is critical. Even as a benchtop tool, the table saw needs an acceptable run-in area with a run-out area the same length. If you do a lot of sheet work—plywood panels, for example—you need greater table size.

Power Tools

Always make sure there is enough clear foot space around the saw, front and rear, to make handling material safe. Move any extension cords, air hoses, board ends, or any other kind of clutter to another area.

- **Minimum table saw space**—about 6' wide by 8' deep, though not necessarily in a block. Rips require only a pass up the center, near the blade, so a plus-sign shape can work, with the 6' width on the horizontal fence bar.
- **Standard 8' board length ripping**—allow 9' in front of the saw and 8' in back of the rear rip fence support. The need for space is not permanent—the saw may be backed up to a door when not in use.

Table Saw Blade Types

A good quality blade will greatly enhance the performance of your saw. For the small shop, a top quality general or combination blade can fit most tasks, but a blade designed for each job is often a better bet. Start with basic rip and crosscut blades.

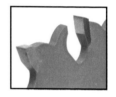

Rip blades cut with the grain and remove a great deal of wood, often on a long cut. They give a clean, reasonably smooth finish cut for glue-ups. Their gullets are deep with room for lots of material to escape from the kerf.

Teeth: Flat top grind (FTG) to chisel wood out. 24, 30, or 40 teeth in a 10"-diameter blade.

Tips: Try a thin kerf blade with a low horsepower saw. Because it takes great power to rip cut, a thin kerf blade makes rip cuts on a low horsepower saw easier.

Crosscut blades cut across the grain in shorter cuts.

Teeth: Alternate top bevel (ATB) grind, 60 to 80 teeth in a 10"-diameter blade. A 10-degree hook allows a fast feed.

Combination blades are single blades that both crosscut and rip well by using a series of tips with small gullets, followed by a deep gullet. The deep gullet cleans out the kerf on rip cuts, while the small gullets between cutting tips help to produce a smooth cut. Combination blades can save you a lot of time that might be lost in changing blades.

Teeth: The alternate top bevel with raker (ATB + R) grind consists of a pair of alternately beveled tips, followed by a flat raker tip.

Tips: Ripping is limited to relatively slow feeds and to woods 2" thick and thinner.

General purpose blades crosscut and rip well, similar to combination blades. Gullets are deep, almost as deep as a rip blade's, and allow for higher feed speeds during rips. Like combination blades, general purpose blades can save the small shop woodworker time that might be lost in changing blades.

Teeth: A typical 10"-diameter blade has 40 teeth with an ATB grind.

Melamine blades help to alleviate the problems with cutting melamine—its abrasiveness and its toughness on saw blades. Also, melamine will chip badly if a good blade isn't used.

Teeth: The blades that best handle melamines (and veneers) come in 60 and 80 tooth versions. They use an ATB grind.

Tips: The more teeth there are, the smoother the cut is; however, the cut must be shallower.

Power Tools

CHAPTER 5

Laminate blades cut laminates and MDF (medium density fiberboard) well. Melamine blades can also work if needed. Generally, it's best to get a true laminate blade if you're doing much work with laminates.

Teeth: The ATB grind changes to a modified TCG (triple chip grind)—one tooth is ground flat on top, the next tooth is ground with an angle at each edge and a flat center, making for lower edge tear-out.

Tips: They can be too aggressive in feed to work well with slide miter saws.

Molding cutter heads are useful for shaping wood and can remove large amounts of wood in a single pass, but they are hard to find. They can be an economical way to produce short runs of small moldings.

Miter Saws

While slide compound miter saws are easy to keep in adjustment, they don't completely supplant radial arm saws in the home or pro shop. The radial arm saw offers a power take off for other tools, handles a dado set, and rips and crosscuts; however, radial arm saws are not widely available.

The knuckle/lever action miter saws from Bosch offer a cut width as wide as the Craftsman 10" radial arm saw—15½"—and sets up, transports, and adjusts more easily. The 12" slide compound miter saws are lighter but harder to adjust than the lever type. Many slide compound miter saws and the lever action saws bevel cut in both directions. Chop action miter saws, regardless of blade size, have quite limited crosscut width; 12" blades cut to the same depth as do those on the slide compound miter saws. Miter saws are more easily portable than radial arm saws.

Cutting Capacity
Consider the compound cut capacity when choosing a slide compound miter saw. Compound cut capacities range from maximum cuts of 2" thick by 8" wide to cuts 3⅛" thick by 12" wide.

Power
For most shops, 13 to 15 amps is plenty.

Blade Capacity
The blade capacity helps to determine the saw's cutting capacity. Blade sizes run from 10" to 12" generally, and there are both dual and single compound models. A 10"-diameter blade should allow you to cut most woods.

Power Tools

Space Requirements

Sliding compound miter saws can be set near a wall. Place the saw in, or near, the center of a wall that is occupied mostly by workbenches to get close to the 16' overall length needed. Having less distance on each side is fine in small shops.

Other Features

You may also want to opt for a comfortable D handle (in vertical and horizontal models), an easy trigger control, and easy adjustments (up front controls are best).

Blades

When looking for blades, get a good quality, at least 60 tooth, ATB (alternate top bevel) blade to start. The bevel (side-to-side) angle on the ATB tips is 20°, making an HATB, or high alternate tip bevel. A 10" blade should handle most jobs; 12" blades can cut crown molding standing up.

Teeth: Tooth counts up to 96 in 12" slide miter saw blades and 80 in 10" blades are good.

Material: For woodworking, carbide is the tip material of choice. For cutting wood that might have metal inclusions, such as nails, a relatively cheap, noncarbide blade is a better sacrifice than a pricey carbide blade. When buying carbide blades, get C4 carbide tips, C3 minimum. Super fine micro-grain carbide takes and holds a very sharp edge. C4 is used only in premium blades.

Plunge Cut Track Saws

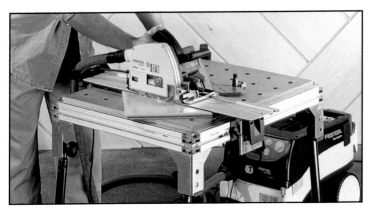

A saw recently being adopted by many woodworkers and do-it-yourselfers, the plunge cut track saw is a hand-held circular saw, designed to work in conjunction with a long, straight rail. To use the tool, you place the track exactly along the desired cut line, and then place the saw atop the rail. It aligns itself. You then just make the cut. The saw tracks perfectly on the rail, so you get a straight cut. In addition, there is no need to clamp the rail in place—it has rubber pads on the bottom that prevent it from wandering. For many DIYers who lack the space for a table saw, this is an alternative. Many professionals use it in place of a dedicated panel saw or as an easy-to transport job-site saw. It is most handy for cutting sheet goods.

Size

The rails are available in 32", 42", 55", 75", 95", 106", 118", and 197" lengths. This allows you to accommodate virtually any size project, although most woodworkers would probably be content with the 106" to rip sheets of plywood and a 55" for crosscutting them.

Space Requirements

Part of the beauty of the system is that it requires very little space, and it can be quickly and easily set up anywhere with a pair of sawhorses and an electrical outlet. When using sawhorses, some form of support is needed to keep the sheet material from sagging. I usually use a couple of 2x4s for material that is under ¾" thick.

Blades

The blades ensure zero tear-out of the material, which means a better result with less sanding. Several manufacturers make blades specifically for plunge cut saws, including Freud, Forrest, and Festool.

Other Features

Like most conventional saws, the blade can be angled to produce beveled cuts.

Band Saws

Band saws are exceptionally useful tools, providing the ability to cut modest curves and to resaw fairly wide boards. Most 14" band saws resaw a 6"-wide board. Some woodworkers use a band saw in place of a table saw.

Size

Band saw size is variable. The most common sizes for hobby shops are 12" and 14". Many band saws sit in a space about 18" x 18". A mobile base will increase that size a bit.

Space Requirements

You'll generally want to have 4' from the table on the sides and the front of the saw. The back may be against the wall because you can't run material in that direction, unless you're cutting long, looping curves that run around behind the machine.

Power Tools

CHAPTER 5

Drill Presses

Drill presses for the small shop come in two versions—benchtop and floor-mounted.

Drilling Capacity

Floor-mounted 15" and larger drill presses do just about anything a small shop woodworker wants, from drilling tiny, precise ³⁄₆₄" holes on up to drilling 3' long ½" holes in hardwood lamp bases. Benchtop drill models tend to be smaller, so their capacities are less than floor-mounted models'.

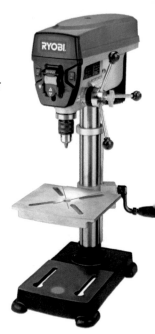

Space Requirements

Benchtops can take less than 14" square on any bench. They can also be set to the back of the bench, or forward with the head reversed to handle longer projects. Place the floor-mounted drill press on a wall slightly in advance of other tools of similar table height—and remember it is the table height that is adjusted on a floor drill press.

- **For an average floor-mounted drill press**—3' on each side, plus 3' in front.
- **For drilling holes near the ends of 6' boards**—at least 5½' from the nearest obstruction on each side.

Power Tools

Benchtop Mortisers

Benchtop mortisers, also called hollow-chisel mortisers, speed the cutting of mortises in almost any wood, within a limited size range. U.S. models are 115 volt, with amperages from 4 to 6. Common rpm may be 1740, which reduces tool burn-out, or 3400, which reduces the time needed to produce a mortise. Motors are all in the heads, and a lever lowers the head, with mortise chisel/drill in place.

Grinders

Some grinders, such as angle grinders, perform heavier-duty rough cutting. Benchtop grinders are often used to sharpen tools. Grinders may be mounted on benches or on pedestals.

Space Requirements

Size variations here are fairly small, but you need a few feet on each side of the grinder, plus 3' in front for the operator. Some pedestal grinders can be set in close, with 1' on either side, but the grinders are light enough to be pulled out and the grinding wheels dressed or changed as required that way.

- **For a pedestal grinder (7" or 8")**—leave 3' on each side.
- **For a benchtop grinder (6")**—leave 1' on each side.

Power Tools

CHAPTER 5

Planers

The planer is less essential in the shop than some other tools because lumber can be bought planed to size. In recent years, a number of companies have come out with 12", 13", and 15" lightweight planers that do an incredible job. Professional shops need planers, usually sizable ones.

Capacity
Portable planers generally take boards up to 12" in width; full-size planers can often take boards up to 20" in width.

Horsepower
Smaller, portable planers can have 15 amp motors. Larger, full-size planers can go all the way up to 10 hp motors.

Feed Rate
Feed rate is measured in feet per minute. The slower the feed, the smoother the board surface. Portable planers tend to have feed rate around $^{20}/_{30}$; full-size planers can be around $^{25}/_{46}$.

Space Requirements

Planers require a long run-in and run-out space. For tight shop spaces, set a planer in front of a door, placing it on a bench or stand that allows you to use the table saw table as a run-out area.

Because board lengths are typically 10' or 12' in length, you can handle much of the work from one side. Individual 1" x 6" or 1" x 8" boards aren't exceptionally heavy, so working from the side is no problem for most people. Take strength into consideration, however—if you can't safely handle the board, find another way.

Lead-in space needs to cover an 18" wide area, so lead-in and run-out space is whatever length you expect your boards to be, plus about 20" for a small planer.

- **For floor mount planers in larger sizes**—add as much as 2'.
- **For most hobby shop planers**—you need about 18" wide (plus a bit for the sides) and 18' to 30' long.
- **For portable planers**—use a cross shape with one very long crossbar. Make sure there's plenty of room to work safely. You should have 12' leading into the planer and 3' to the adjustment side of the planer. A 27' space works well for accepting the boards coming out of the planer.

CHAPTER 5

Jointers

Jointers are essential for power tool shops. They flatten the first face of wood, and then create an edge at 90 degrees to that face, giving the vital square edge. The jointer is a tool that can kick back, and your fingers are working exceptionally close to the spinning blades. The guards must be in use and in good shape.

Capacity
Smaller benchtop jointers can take boards about 6" in width; larger jointers can often take boards up to 12" in width.

Horsepower
Smaller jointers tend to have 1 hp motors. Larger models typically have 3 hp motors.

Space Requirements

Most material cleaned up on a jointer is fairly short, and most hobby jointers don't do a good job on material over about 60". Add that to a tool that seldom measures 72" long, and you need a length of 10'. The space needed for the width also isn't as great—12" width for 6" blade width jointers, plus enough room for you to stand alongside the jointer and feed the material through. Jointers are easily wheeled around on mobile bases.

The space required is small, because most hobby shop jointers are under a foot wide, with blade widths from 4" to 8", and less than 74" long. Some are light enough to be easily moved, so that they can be placed against another tool and lifted or pulled into place for use when you need them. Like most power tools, jointers get more use when they occupy their own slots.

- **The average jointer** needs 6' in front, 6' in back, and 3' to one side of the jointer, plus the size of the jointer.
- **A 60"-long jointer** with 24" of space at each end works well and is less than 9' of permanent space assigned.

CHAPTER 5

Lathes

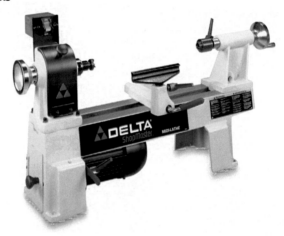

The lathe is the artist's tool extraordinaire. The lathe bed is the base of the tool and may be of cast iron, steel tubing, or other material, usually in two parallel rails. Cast iron is generally considered better than tubing. The more solid the bed is, the more accurate the lathe can be. The lathe sits on a stand or a heavy bench. Overall, the heavier the lathe, the easier it is to make precise turnings. Weight also dampens vibration.

Parts of the Lathe
- The **ways** are the machined parts of the bed on which the tools rest and the tailstock moves.
- The **headstock** is at the left end of the bed and may also contain the motor housing. The motor may also be hung on the outside of the headstock.
- The **driving center**, with spur, attaches to an arbor that holds a pulley. The pulley attaches, through a series of belts, to the motor.
- The **tailstock** is at the far end of the lathe on the right. This part can be moved along the base rails to vary the distance between the back center and the driving center so different length materials can be turned.

Power Tools

- The **back center** is on the spindle at the top inside left of the tailstock, facing the driving center.
- The **spindle lock** and spindle advance are located on the tailstock to lock pieces in place for turning.
- The **tailstock lock** is usually located under the tailstock between the rails.
- The **spindle** on the tailstock holds the tailstock center.
- The **tool rest** is located between the tailstock and the headstock. This adjustable platform that comes in several shapes is where the turner rests the turning tool as it shaves away material.
- The **tool rest lock** locks the rest in place with the height and distance from the work desired.

Speed

Swap the belts from pulley to pulley to raise and lower driving center speed. Older lathes have driving speeds ranging from 500 to 3000 rpm, depending on pulley size, arrangement, and other factors. Some newer lathes do not use belts; instead they have an electronic speed control that is both faster and safer to use.

Space Requirements

Lathes are another tool that can be backed against a wall and left in place. Lathes require some light plywood or sheet metal work to duct their wastes to a dust collecting system.

- **For most lathes**—Leave 4' to the left (at the head stock) and 3' in front along the entire length of the bed for the operator's stance. Because most hobby lathes are not much longer than 3' at the bed and 5' to 6' overall, a space of 9' or 10' along the wall works.
- **If you're using a bowl lathe**—move it out from the wall to allow yourself access around large bowls. Station this type of lathe at least 4' from any wall on the working end.

CHAPTER 5

Routers

This do-everything tool router joints, produces decorative edges, makes internal sign and other cuts, works to patterns from templates, makes many kinds of molding, makes cuts to produce raised panel doors, makes cuts for the rails and stiles for those doors, and many other things. The router is a motor with a collet

(performs a lot like a drill chuck) on one end, and a base surrounding the barrel. A switch provides power, and the collet holds a bit in place.

For small capacity work, Dremel's variety of small-motor tools is useful. It is similar to a drill, or a router, using collects in three sizes to accept tools ranging from very small to tiny. The tool can grind, saw, carve, and cut with appropriate attachments. Dremel also sells a flex shaft tool that is useful for any kind of intricate work, such as that found in carving. Foredom Electric sells a power head and flex shaft tool, as well as a long, long list of tools useful to power carvers.

Laminate trimmers are the lightweights, though they can serve as onehanded routers, as well as trimming laminate to whatever angle a job needs. These small, slender units are available with different types of bases, including straight locked, offset, and tilt. Kits may include a power unit, case, and two or three different bases. Most are around 5 or 6 amperes in power, have ¼" collets, and have speeds in the 30,000-rpm range.

Plunge router heads mount on two posts that are part of the base. This type of router wears out faster than those with fixed bases. Plunge routers are superb for making interior cuts for mortises, stopped dadoes, or any operation where the router needs to start its own hole.

Motor Speed

Motor speeds on routers vary from a low of 8,000 rpm to as high as 30,000 rpm. Variable speeds let you match speed to router bit size (the bigger the bit's cutting diameter, the slower the speed used), wood density, and hardness.

Horsepower

Lighter routers, such as ¾ hp, 1 hp, and 1½ hp, are easy for the novice. Depending on actual power and product quality, motors on fixed base routers under 1½ hp are often 8 amperes or less. For serious long-term woodworking, begin at 1½ hp. Plunge routers start at 1¼ hp and rise to 3½ hp. More power means more weight and bulk. Large routers work in router tables to form raised panels.

Bit Capacity

Routers generally take ¼" bits. Larger routers that can use ¼" or ½" bits are able to perform heavier cutting with ease.

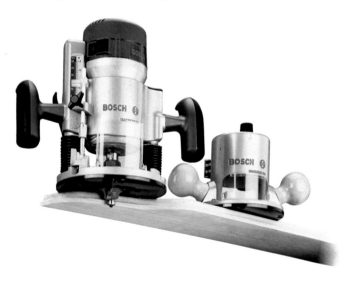

Shaper and Router Tables

Router tables are very versatile and can be used for a number of tasks, including joinery and trim. While router tables do much the same job as shapers and may provide a smoother finish because of higher speeds, they are not totally interchangeable. Router tables and power feeders don't mesh well, nor do router tables and very large pattern raised panels. As a heavy-duty tool, the shaper excels at performing heavier cuts. Router tables are light-duty tools compared to even a small, 2 hp shaper, but they can be exceptionally useful for the hobbyist and for smaller jobs in the small pro shop.

Space Requirements

The space needs of both shapers and router tables are similar. A large operator movement area is needed because both router tables and shapers are often used to shape pieces that extend towards the operator a considerable distance—door panel tops, sides, and bottoms. Leave space behind and around the tool for adjustments and bit changes and space in front of the tool for operation.

- For making molding—Leave long run-in and run-out space.
- Ideal space—6' of working space for the operator, plus 8' from the table on each end.

Power Tools

Bits

There is a bit for every routing task, from simple grooves to intricate moldings. In fact, there are hundreds of cutters available in a variety of profiles and widths. The pages that follow feature a selection of router bits along with the cuts they make.

Router bits can be divided into three groups according to their size and function. Edge-forming bits rout decorative profiles in the edges of a workpiece or cut one or both halves of an interlocking joint. Edge-forming bits generally have a ball-bearing pilot located below the cutter that rides along the edge of the workpiece to guide the bit and precisely control the width of the cut. As their name implies, grooving bits are designed to cut grooves and dadoes, and work best in a plunge router.

Finally, the bits shown last are larger than standard bits and should be used with the router mounted in a router table. Many router bits are expensive, so store them carefully and use a clean cloth to wipe off pitch, dust, and dirt after each use. Keep the cutting edges sharp and avoid using bits that are dirty, rusted, or damaged.

Edge-Forming Bits

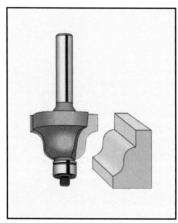

Roman ogee bit

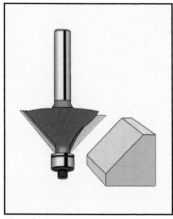

Chamfer bit

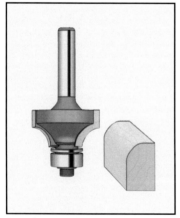

Rounding-over bit

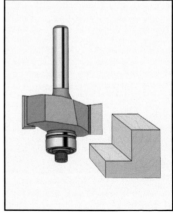

Rabbet bit

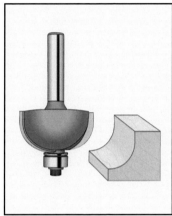

Cove bit

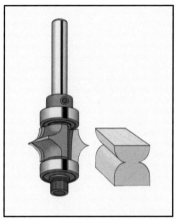

Double-piloted full bead bit

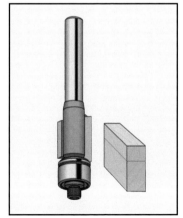

Flush-cutting bit

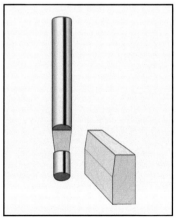

Bevel-trimming bit

Power Tools

Grooving Bits

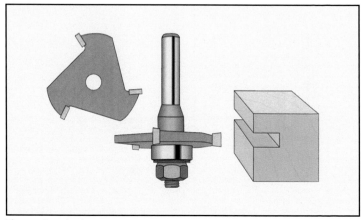

Three-wing slotting cutter

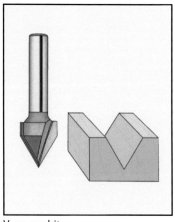

V-groove bit

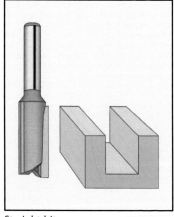

Straight-bit

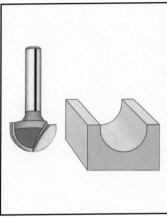

Core box bit

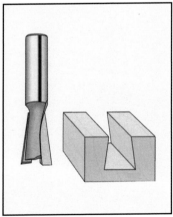

Dovetail bit

CHAPTER 5

Router Table Bits

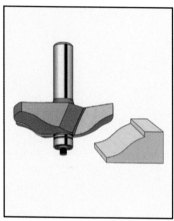

Standard panel-raising bit

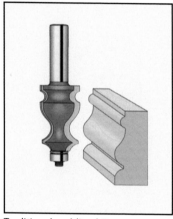

Traditional molding bit

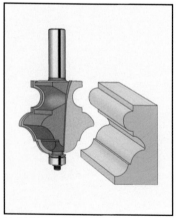

Multi-bit

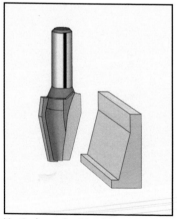

Vertical panel-raising bit

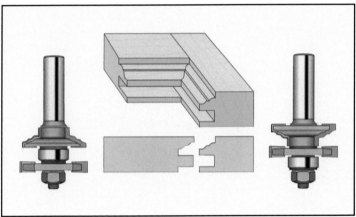

Coping bit   Sticking bit

Power Tools

Router Feeding Direction

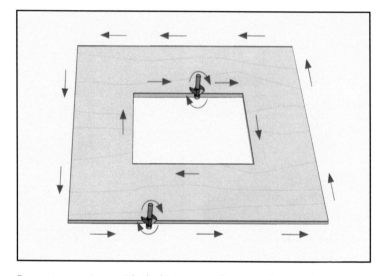

For most operations, guide the bit into a workpiece against the direction of the bit rotation; this will pull the bit into the wood. On an outside edge, move the router in a counter-clockwise direction; on an inside edge, feed the tool clockwise as shown. Start with cuts that are against the grain so you can eliminate any tearout with the cuts along the grain that follow. Position yourself to pull the router toward you, rather than pushing the tool.

Air Compressors

Vertical tank compressors are best buys for a stationary unit in the woodworking shop. Use a 60- or 80-gallon tank and a 5 hp or larger motor. Small tanks on portable units cannot carry the load with spray guns, sanders, and sandblasters, but they work well with staplers, brad nailers, and finish nailers. Oiled compressors are quieter and more durable than oil-free, but cost more.

The size of the tank and its power must be mated to the work to be done for satisfactory work. Light-duty compressors with small tanks are superb for anything up to a 15 gauge finish nailer. Pancake compressors are especially popular because of their compactness. With framing and roofing nailers, a single nail gun on a small compressor works well. Several small brad nailers or staplers can be run at the same time. Sanding and painting will prove nearly impossible as tank pressure drops and then cycles up too often for smooth work.

Single stage air compressors are limited to about 125 to 150 pounds per square inch (psi) pressure. Two-stage air compressors get a final compression stage that raises pressures to about 175 psi, with greater standard cubic feet per minute (scfm) delivery at a particular psi.

Capacity Requirements

It pays to target uses before buying any air compressor. When checking the scfm, find out what the psi is for that output. Getting 12 scfm at 40 psi won't work for a tool that needs 10 scfm at 90 psi. Good, basic two-stage units will yield 16 scfm or more at 90 psi. A top end single stage may struggle to give 10 scfm at 90 psi. As noted, pneumatic sanders and spray guns for finishes are among the heavy load capacity types.

- **Typical random orbit sander:** 7 scfm
- **Brad nailer:** 0.95 scfm
- **Most sanders:** between 3 scfm and 7 scfm
- **High-pressure spray guns:** 10 scfm
- **15-gauge finish nailer:** 1.5 scfm

Dust Collection

Dust collectors are the first line of lung protection. The recognition of wood dust as a possible carcinogen is an excellent reason for collection. Varying degrees of allergic reactions also need to be considered and dust masks may also be required. There are literally dozens of pipes and tubing and fittings that work with various collectors, making a collection assembly easier.

Categories of Collection

Shop vacuums use a small diameter hose, no more than 2 or 2½ inches, and a noisy universal motor.

Single-stage dust collectors use induction motors that are quiet and durable with an upper bag to filter fine dust and a lower bag to collect regular dust, bits, and pieces.

Power Tools

Two-stage dust collectors use a drum, placed so that chips and larger objects drop into the drum before they strike impeller blades; fine dust collects in a filter bag.

Cyclone units create airflow that separates out the dust and chips, dropping all but the finest dust into a container at the base of the cyclone; super fine dust is collected in a bag; can be used with single or two-stage collectors to increase efficiency.

Air cleaners fit near the ceiling and use a series of filters that trap particles too small for other collectors; used to collect anything dust collector units leave behind.

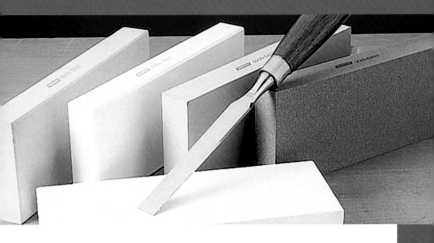

Important Sharpening Skills

One of the most useful skills for a woodworker is the ability to quickly put an edge on a cutting tool. There are generally two ways to do the job, wet or dry, and the tools range from stones to power tools to sandpaper on a flat surface.

CHAPTER 6

Wet vs. Dry

There are two basic categories of actual sharpening processes—wet and dry. With the dry method, there is considerable amount of metal dust, which, for wise woodworkers means wearing a dust mask. In the wet method, the water or oil carries away the dust that settles in and around the sandpaper in the dry method.

Sharpening tools and materials

The tools and materials you choose for sharpening will largely depend on your needs and preferences—one type is not necessarily better than another.

Abrasive paper

Using abrasive paper to sharpen tools can be a wet or dry process. Both produce great edges. Take a few strips of micron abrasive paper or wet-and-dry sandpaper from 400 to 2000 grit, a flat plate, and some spray-on adhesive, and you're ready to go.

Stones

Using stones is another way to produce a good edge. Some stones can only be used with a wet sharpening process.

Stone Type	Lubricant Needed	Rate of Wear	Rate of Cutting	Available Grits	Durability	Other Notes
Oil	Oil	Wears quickly	Quickly	Many	Durable	Easy-to-flatten, oil can stain wood
Water	Water	Wears very quickly	Very quickly	Very many	Fragile	Can cause tools to rust
Ceramic	None	Wears slowly	Slowly	Limited	Fragile	Load quickly
Diamond	None	Wears slowly	Quickly	Limited	Durable	—

Diamond hones clean up and sharpen flat surfaces on drill and router bits.

Burnishers are typically long, hardened steel rods with handles and are used to sharpen scrapers.

Power Tools

Using power tools for sharpening produces good results and speeds up the process. Power tools can be used for both the wet and dry categories of sharpening.

- **Grinders**—Most grinders use a grinding wheel, which is set either vertically or horizontally. Horizontal grinders can be difficult to use because the inside of the wheel spins faster than the outside. Wheels come in different grits and need to be dressed as they wear. Some horizontal grinders take adhesive disks, which eliminates the need to dress a wheel.

- **Belt sanders**—In addition to their uses in sanding, belt sanders can also prove useful for sharpening. Belts are available in a wide variety of grits that aren't available for grinding wheels.

Methods of Sharpening

As with most woodworking jobs, sharpening can be done in many different ways. The method I'm offering here, which uses abrasive paper, is one of the easiest to learn and keep up for many hand tools. This method of sharpening is often called Scary Sharp™.

1. Attach a few strips of micron abrasive paper or wet-and-dry sandpaper, from 400 to 2000 grit, to a flat plate glass using spray adhesive. (For more information on flat surfaces, see the next section.) To ease the strain of holding the correct angle, a good quality holder is a useful accessory.
2. If you're starting with a new chisel or plane iron, flatten the back first. (If you are using Japanese chisels, do not flatten the back; they're designed to have a fork up the center of the back, which is forged in).
3. Start with 15 micron paper (1000 grit) or 400 to 600 grit wet and dry, used to remove factory or toolbox induced scratches.
4. Follow with a 5 micron (about 2500 grit) for a few strokes, until any scratches left from the 15 micron paper are gone.
5. Set up the proper angle for the tool you're sharpening. (Use a jig if desired.)
6. Sharpen through the grits. Start with about a 600 grit and go up to 4000. Don't try to go from 600 to 2000; the intermediate steps are necessary to reduce scratch size from the previous grit. When using micro-abrasives, start with 400- or 600-grit wet or dry paper; then go through 15 micron, 5 micron, and .5 micron.

CHAPTER 6

Finding a Flat Surface

Be sure to get as flat a surface as you can find. I use a 2" thick granite plate and two 8½" x 14" sheets of tempered glass. Because both of these are fragile, you'll want to treat them with care. Unfinished Medium Density Fiberboard (MDF) is sturdy, tough, and inexpensive, making it very suitable for a flat backing.

Final Honing or Stropping

The final honing of any edged tool can be done with a leather strop. Make your own, or buy one, and use it with a good honing compound in the .5 micron range. After a few strokes, you'll be able to cut anything the tool is meant to cut.

Sharpening Scrapers

Scrapers are easier to sharpen than many other tools, requiring just a flat file and a burnisher. Clamp the scraper in a vise with just the top inch or so showing. Use the file to file it flat. Then, use the burnisher to turn the wire edges that form.

Sharpening Handsaws

To sharpen a handsaw, clamp it between two boards using your vise, keeping the boards just below the bottoms of the teeth. Use a triangular file to sharpen the teeth and a saw set to make sure you have the correct set on every tooth.

Sharpening Angles

For most chisels and plane iron uses, maintaining the standard angle is easiest and works best. There is a range, though, and experimentation over time lets you develop your preferences.

Tool	Cutting Angle	Bevel	Back Bevel	Relief Angle
Block plane, standard	35°	15°	10°	10°
Block plane, low angle	32°	20°	5°	7°
Bench plane	Not Significant	45° (softwood) 50° (hardwood)	NA	NA
General use bevel edge chisel	NA	25° (use 30° on narrow chisels, 20° on wide)	NA	NA
Paring chisels	NA	20°, 15° for fine work	NA	NA
Mortising chisels	NA	30° for softwood; 35° for hardwood	NA	NA
Drawknife	NA	35°	5°	NA
Carving gouge	NA	25° (starting point)	5° (if used)	NA
Roughing gouge (lathe)	NA	45°	NA	NA
Bowl gouge	NA	40° (starting point)	NA	NA
Spindle gouge	NA	25°	NA	NA
Skew (70°)	NA	12½ to 15° each side (do both sides)	NA	NA
Parting tool	NA	30° to 50°	NA	NA
Cabinet scrapers	NA	90° burnish off wire edge after filing (5 to 10° burnishing angle)	NA	NA

Handsaw Tooth Filing Angles

Set is the width from the center of the blade to the outside tip of the tooth. **Rake** is the angle from the vertical of the saw blade.

These tables are meant as guides only. Use your own working habits to finalize any angles used.

Tool	Rake	Set
Ripsaw	0°	½ tooth thickness
Crosscut, standard	30° both sides	½ tooth thickness
Crosscut, aggressive	15° front	½ tooth thickness

Basics of Wood Finishing

The finish is the last step of a wood project and the first thing most people notice when they view the piece. What is not noticed is the work that goes into prepping before the finish goes on.

Finishes provide protection for the underlying material; provide ways to change color, add sheen, bring out chatoyance, and enhance the characteristics of the wood; and can hide the characteristics of the wood. A good finish is more than just buying a product in a can—you'll need to have a clear sense of the look and feel you're striving for, and how the finish will need to perform in a practical sense. You can then consider the various types of finishing products available and their application methods so that you can choose wisely. Before applying any finishes, however, you'll need to prep the wood with a careful sanding.

CHAPTER 7

Safety Tips

Gloves. A good pair of chemical-resistant gloves is a must to protect your skin from harmful chemicals.

Eyewear. Any type of eyewear with side protection works well for any splashing that might occur.

Mask or Respirator. Always use an appropriate type of mask to protect yourself from finishing fumes.

Rag Disposal. When using oil finishes, make sure all rags are handled safely. Do not stack them in piles! Soak them in water; then hang and dry them before discarding. Rags that are not handled properly can spontaneously combust.

Abrasives

The first step in finishing is often smoothing wood with abrasives in preparation for a finish.

Backings. Abrasives are backed with cloth or paper. Cloth is more durable than paper. Use heavyweight cloth (X) or lightweight (J) depending on need. Paper comes in more grades, from A through F, F being the heaviest. Lighter papers are used with finer grits.

Open Coat vs. Closed Coat Abrasives

- **Open coat abrasives** are applied to 50% to 70% of the backing surface. If resinous woods are sanded, open coat papers are usually needed.
- **Closed coat abrasives** completely coat the surface. These abrasives cut faster with woods that don't load up the paper. Zinc stearate may be added to keep the paper from gumming up; however, stearates may interfere with finish adhesion. A thorough cleaning must follow any stearate paper use.

Grits. Proper surface preparation takes the wood to at least a 150-grit sanding. If the wood is to be painted, 120-grit finish sanding is enough. Some people prefer 180 grit for clear finishes. On bare wood, no more than 220 grit is normally used. Remember that finishes need a tooth, a surface that allows some grip, so don't sand your wood too finely. Finer grits are for sanding between finish coats. Grits for woodworking are as follows:

- **Coarse**—50
- **Medium**—60, 80, 100
- **Fine**—120, 150, 180, 220
- **Extra Fine**—240, 320, 400
- **Wet-and-dry papers**—all of the above, with 600, 800, 1000, and 1200 added to extra fine.

Micro-abrasive grits are available and useful for a wide variety of work. The rough stuff is 15 micron, equivalent to about 1000 grit; 5 micron is about 2500 grit; and 0.5 micron is approximately 9000 grit. These are useful for sharpening tools, as well as for producing high gloss finishes on wood.

Types of Abrasives

- **Garnet** works best for hand sanding. Its very sharp grit holds sharpness by fracturing in use.
- **Aluminum oxide** is sharp, durable, and mostly used for machine sanding.
- **Silicon carbide** comes in wet and dry types—very dark gray for wet and light gray for dry. It is a preferred abrasive for rubbing out dried finishes and for sanding between coats.
- **Alumina-zirconia** is used for heavy surfacing operations, such as those carried out in drum sanders. Its grains also fracture, keeping a fresh surface available.
- **Steel wool** is an abrasive for woodworking, most often for creating an eggshell (matte) finish from a glossier finish. The specific grade used for such work is 0000, or 4-0. Coarser versions down to a #1 are available and useful for knocking down raised grain early in finishing. For water-based finishes, use some of the abrasive pads to avoid rust marks.

Repairing Surface Damage

Flaws on a wood surface can show through almost any finish. In fact, a clear finish like lacquer may magnify imperfections. Before you apply a finish to a piece of furniture, you need to find and mend any surface damage. Most defects stick out, but you need to find and eliminate the less obvious blemishes as well. Try running a hand across the wood and feeling for them. You can also wash the surface with low angle light and look for them.

The best approach to a repair and the materials required depend on the nature of the damage. A suitable repair for a dent, for example, is to lift it with steam. However, if the wood fibers are severed rather than simply crushed, steam will not work; a wood filler may be the best remedy.

You can buy special burn-in kits for applying shellac sticks. The typical package includes a burn-in knife with a gently bent, stainless steel blade; an alcohol lamp for heating the knife; and a special solution for soaking a felt block that levels the repair with the surrounding surface.

Most larger blemishes are best concealed with wood filler. Although many types are pre-colored, you can create a custom color by mixing two or more together. Test the filler on a scrap of the target wood before committing yourself to a particular formulation. In situations where a filler is inappropriate because the damaged area is too large or the filler would be conspicuous, you can mend the defect with a shop-made patch fashioned from a wood scrap of the same species.

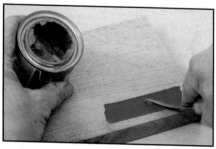

Most modern patching compounds are formulated to be chemically compatible with a variety of finishes, but in cases where the two products contain the same solvent, the finish can dissolve the filler.

For all your fixes, whether lifting a dent or filling a gouge, lightly sand the repair once you are done to level it with the surrounding surface.

Tip: Most fillers are compatible with most finishes, and many can even accept stain reasonably well. Just to be on the safe side, however, you'll want to do a trial run once the filler on your scrap piece has dried. Coat it with stain and then wipe it off as per the manufacturer's instructions. You can then see if the stained area will blend in well enough with the wood. If not, you can mix fillers differently until you get a result you're happy with.

Tip: In addition to the kind of filler discussed here, which is applied prior to the finish, recent years have seen the introduction of a second kind of filler which can be pressed into defects after the finish goes on. This is particularly useful in architectural applications—for example, when you're attaching moldings in a home and want to fill the nail holes. Once the woodwork has been stained, it is a snap to mix a custom color that matches the trim and the nail holes will just disappear. This kind of filler never fully hardens, so it must not be used beneath a finish coat.

Categories of Finish

Finishes can be divided into two categories: penetrating finishes and film-forming finishes. These names are pretty self-explanatory: oil finishes fall into the first category, and polyurethanes and lacquers fall into the latter.

Penetrating Finishes

Pros:

- Easy to apply—just flood the surface, let it soak in, and wipe away the excess
- Easy to maintain—if the finish gets damaged over time, just apply another coat
- User-friendly—some are even safe for kids toys

Cons:

- Dull appearance which may not look as rich
- Must be refreshed periodically (typically once per year or more)

Film-Forming Finishes

Pros:

- Resists wear—well-suited to high-use surfaces
- Easy to clean—just wipe down or use regular household cleansers
- Offers varying levels of sheen which bring out wood's richness
- Can be easy to apply—wiping polyurethanes offer the simplicity of oils, for example

Cons:

- Poor application can leave brushmarks or other surface defects
- Some finishes (i.e. lacquers) can be smelly and require lots of ventilation

Lacquer

Characteristics: Leaves a thin, clear coating and forms a protective film. Final form is elastic. Comes in gloss, semi-gloss, and flat.

Best Application: Spray
Drying Time: Fast
Repair: Easily repaired
Strengths: Highly resistant to most spills. Does not go soft in high temperatures.
Weaknesses: Some solvents (acetone) eat right through lacquers. Water marks develop with too much moisture. Not easily brushed because of fast drying time, but there are specially formulated brushing lacquers.
Best Uses: Production environments, for example, spraying a large number of cabinet doors.
Tips: Match lacquer and thinner brands. Use a sealer coat over any wood filler applied.

Varnish

Characteristics: Oleo-resinous varnishes contain oil and synthetic resins. Tung oil varnish is tung oil combined with driers to decrease drying time. Boiled linseed oil varnish is similar to tung oil varnish. Tung oil varnish is more durable.

Best Application: Brush, spray, or rag
Drying Time: Slow
Repair: Difficult.
Strengths: Easier to brush on than lacquers, more useful in small shops. Can be reduced with inexpensive thinners. Easy to apply. Tough. Durable. High water resistance. Some made for exterior use.
Weaknesses: Bubbles form when brushing (thin 10% to 20% to reduce); skin forms in the can. Can be difficult to rub out.
Best Uses: Furniture and other projects that require a durable, easy-to-clean topcoat.
Tips: Be very careful of dust, as varnish can take more than an hour to dry tack-free.

Basics of Wood Finishing

Spar Varnish

Characteristics: Uses tung oil and phenolic resin for flexible finish for outdoor and marine use. Ultraviolet inhibitors may be added. Available in satin and gloss.

Best Application: Brush or pad
Drying Time: Slow. Tack-free time is more than one hour.
Repair: Difficult.
Strengths: Deals well with changes in moisture content and temperature. Sands easily.
Weaknesses: Somewhat difficult to apply. Fairly soft. Not good for table tops or high abrasion areas. Moderately difficult to brush.
Best Uses: Outdoor projects, to combat the effects of weather and UV rays.
Tips: Use where an object will be in temperature extremes. Spar varnish is softer than standard varnish and flexes more without damage, so is used outdoors.

Gel Varnish

Characteristics: Designed for easy application. Not as durable as standard varnishes, but appealing because of easy application.

Best Application: Rag or pad
Drying Time: Moderate (6 to 12 hours)
Repair: Difficult.
Strengths: Easy to apply.
Weaknesses: Expensive, skin forms in can.
Best Uses: Furniture and a variety of indoor projects.
Tips: Read instructions carefully. Use high quality application materials.

Shellac

Characteristics: Base is secreted by Lac bug (Laccifer lacca). Available colors from dark orange to nearly colorless. Comes in flake form. Alcohol is its solvent. Available ready mixed. Successive coats melt into those below.

Best Application: Brush or rag
Drying Time: Fast
Repair: Easy, because it dissolves itself
Strengths: Completely non-toxic after drying. (It's used to coat many pills.)
Weaknesses: Vulnerable to water and alcohol.
Best Uses: Reproduction furniture, and children's toys because of its nontoxic properties.
Tips: Use dewaxed shellacs as sealers for ther finishes.

Polyurethane

Characteristics: Polyurethane, either water- or oil-based, is coating of choice for kitchen and bathroom cabinetry.

Best Application: Brush, spray, or rag
Drying Time: Varies from a fairly fast six hours to overnight.
Repair: Difficult, often must strip and recoat.
Strengths: Exceptionally durable. Hard. Tough. Water resistant. Perfect for floor use.
Weaknesses: Tends to be brittle; not used when humidity changes expected. Hard to sand.
Best Uses: Projects with kitchen and bathroom cabinetry; good in heavy wear situations.
Tips: Polyurethane varnishes require exceptional care in application, and the second coating must be done within 24 hours or the between-coats bond will not be good.

Topcoat Finishes

In general use, topcoats are the last finish that goes on after primer, stain preventer/killer (e.g., Kilz), or other such coats. In woodworking, topcoats are usually light in color, often clear, and may be any of literally dozens of brands and numerous kinds, ranging from shellac to tung and Danish oils, back to teak oil, and on to lacquers and varnishes. The finishes have different solvents, with shellac requiring alcohol, which makes it susceptible to water damage but makes fixes easy. Simply clean and re-coat. Some topcoats are wipe on, many are brush on, and most may be sprayed if desired.

Clear finishes are generally water-based finishes that dry fast, are easy to clean, are nonflammable, and are nontoxic. They come in several sheens: flat, satin, semigloss, and gloss. Adding substances produces lower gloss. You may also lower the gloss by sanding with 400-grit sandpaper, wet or dry. Steel wool in 0000 grade gives excellent results. Pumice (FF grade) may also be used with a rubbing oil. Follow up with rottenstone. Piano finishes need a bit more: 600-grit wet-and-dry paper; then a good buffing with a top grade paste wax.

Waxes are not finishes. Waxes buff-up and add a rich depth to surfaces. They also provide protection on an already applied finish. You can make your own waxes, using combinations of carnauba, beeswax, and paraffin wax, but use exceptional care when mixing waxes. Do not use an open flame and be very careful of fire. Beeswax is soft and almost sticky. Carnauba is hard. Paraffin or canning wax is intermediate. Using modest amounts of mineral oil, you can formulate almost any hardness and spreadability. Use pigments or dyes to color the waxes, and add perfumes. These waxes can be used to protect cast iron tool tables. You could also use a good paste wax.

Oils

Tung and linseed oils are the two most commonly used oils for finishing. Many woodworkers choose these oils for finishing because they create a natural look. Provided that the finished project is not exposed to frequent contact with water, chemicals, and other such elements, tung and linseed oils give an attractive, easy-to-apply, and easy-to-maintain finish.

- **Boiled linseed oil** provides limited protection against liquids and scratches and yellows over time. Because of raw linseed oil's slow drying time, most woodworkers use boiled linseed oil, which has chemical additives to speed drying.
- **Tung oil** also provides limited protection against liquids and scratches. It yellows less than linseed oil and dries more quickly in its pure state, in as little as six hours.

Solvents for Stains and Finishes

All stains and finishes need a solvent. Water and mineral spirits are the most common solvents. Water works well for some clear finishes and also gives a clearer look than oil-based finishes. Oil-based stains and finishes use turpentine or mineral spirits as their solvents and tend to yellow the wood color. Alcohol is also used as a solvent for numerous finishes and stains. Lacquer thinner thins only lacquer, and it's best to use the lacquer manufacturer's brand of thinner with its brand of lacquer.

Stain and Finish Compatibility

Like does not always work with like; be sure that you know the type of solvent or thinner needed. Mineral spirits in both stain and finish means no compatibility problems. Do not use the same solvent for a finish that was used for a dye stain. Alcohol-based dye stains, for example, go muddy if shellac is wiped or brushed over them. The dye is re-dissolved in the solvent, and the color is ruined.

Stains

Stains color wood, from the color of natural grain to an entirely different color. There are numerous types, each with a coloring agent and vehicle. Generally, stains fall under one of two categories: pigmented stains or dye stains.

Pigment Stains

Any substance that can be reduced to a powder can become a pigment that will impart color to wood. Minerals, ores, metallic oxides and many other naturally occurring earth compounds can all be ground into very fine particles. Once they are suspended in a solvent such as oil, varnish, polyurethane, or water, these powders become spreadable pigment stains. Because the particles are suspended, rather than dissolved in the solution, pigment stains dry to a thin, paint-like coating on the surface of the wood.

Whereas dye stains color wood fibers and tend to accentuate the grain, pigment stains are opaque and hide the wood patterns. As a result, pigment stains are often used for glazing, graining, and other finishing techniques that compensate for the lack of distinct grain patterns in certain varieties of wood.

Today, pigments are produced synthetically, with binders and driers added to help them adhere to the wood as the solvent dries. Pigment stains come in different liquid and gel forms. The most popular and best-known are pigmented wiping stains. These ready-to-use finishing products contain finely ground pigment suspended in linseed oil, which doubles as solvent and binding agent. Wiping stains are slow-drying, allowing plenty of time to spread them on or wipe off any excess. Either sprayed on or applied with a rag or a brush, they are particularly useful when the wood surface is made up of heartwood and contrasting sapwood.

Dye Stains

Derived from plants, insects, and animals, the wood dyes used in the 18th century ranged from concoctions with exotic names such as dragon's blood, verdigris, madder root, and cochineal to more earthy tints extracted from tea, urine, vinegar, and walnut husks. A hundred years later, the first aniline dye was extracted from coal tar. Today, such dyes are the industry standard, usually mixed with one of three solvents: water, oil, or alcohol. Dyes not yet combined with a solvent are also available in either powder or liquid form. Premixed stains are more convenient to use, but mixing them yourself gives you more flexibility when you need to produce a particular effect. A fourth type of dye product, known as non-grain-raising (NGR) stain, is only available in liquid form. The dyes in NGR stains are dissolved in an anhydrous, or waterless, solution of organic hydrocarbons, such as petroleum. Whichever type of dye stain you apply, the factor that will determine the eventual color of the wood is the amount of dye in the solution, not the amount of solution applied.

Water-soluble stains are a good choice for emphasizing the grain of hardwoods. Although a water-based stain will raise the grain, many woodworkers prefer to take care of that step before applying a stain, thereby saving a sanding step that might affect the final color of the wood.

Alcohol-soluble dyes, also called "spirit stains," do not raise the grain as much as water-based stains and they produce somewhat brighter hues.

Oil-soluble dyes are transparent and also non-grain-raising. The drying times of these stains will vary depending on the solvent used. Mineral spirit-based stains generally have a slow drying time, while stains containing toluene or xylene dry considerably faster. The trade-off is that toluene and xylene are more toxic than mineral spirits. Another potential problem with oil-based stains is their tendency to bleed through a protective finish. Although this should only occur if the stain is still wet when the topcoat is applied, it is a good practice nonetheless to use a finish with a different solvent than your stain.

For best results, NGR stains should be sprayed on wood. If you use a brush, you will need to add a retarder to the solution to extend its drying time.

Choosing the right stain for a project can involve experimentation. Illustrated are the effects of five different dye stains on some of the most popular hardwood species. The samples on the far left are unstained, followed by pieces cut from the same board, each one colored by a different dye stain.

Commonly Used Stains

- **Water stains** are dye stains. They apply easily with a brush and raise the wood grain.
- **Oil stains** may be pigment or dye stains. In pigment oil stains, the pigment is added to linseed oil. With dye oil stains, the dye penetrates the wood. Oil stains mix with many types of wood fillers, making staining and filling a one-step process. Oil stains are brushed or wiped on, and then wiped off. Adjust color depth by the amount of time the stain is left on.

- **Spirit stains** are dye stains dissolved in alcohol. Drying is fast, penetration is light. Darker colors need two or more coats. Spirit stains tend to bleed.
- **Gel stains** are wipe-on types and are used with woods where blotching might be a problem—cherry and both soft and hard maple are examples. Gel stains do not penetrate because they do not flow, and therefore are less likely to blotch.

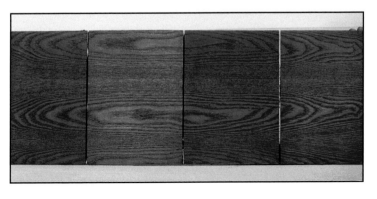

Basics of Wood Finishing

Solvents for Finishes

- **Mineral spirits**, **naphtha**, and **turpentine** are solvents for wax and dye stains. They are thinners for pigment stains, wax, oil, and varnishes.
- **Alcohol** is a solvent for shellac, lacquer finishes, and alcohol-based dye stains. It is also a thinner for shellac and NGR (non-grain raising) dye stains.
- **Lacquer thinner** is a solvent for oil-soluble dye stains, shellac, lacquer, and finishes. It is a thinner for lacquer-based pigment stain, NGR dye stain, lacquer, and catalyzed lacquer.
- **Glycol ether** is a solvent for NGR dye stains, pigment stain, shellac, lacquer, and finishes. It's also a thinner for NGR finishes.
- **Water** is a solvent for water-soluble dye stains and a thinner for finishes and pigment stains.

Bleaching Wood

Bleach is useful for lightening the natural color of the wood or removing stains applied to wood. Be sure to clean and sand the wood lightly before using bleaches. Listed below are a few common types and their uses.

- **Standard chlorine bleach** removes dye stains, but not pigment stains. Use goggles, gloves, and an apron when applying.
- **Oxalic acid** does a good job of removing iron stains (often caused by using ferrous fasteners or steel wool) in oaks. Make sure the iron is removed before using the oxalic acid. Follow manufacturer's directions.
- **A/B bleach** is a two-part package: lye and hydrogen peroxide. It removes ink, water rings, and similar stains that chlorine bleach and oxalic acid won't touch. Use great care and follow the manufacturer's instructions closely. Both substances can be dangerous, so gloves and goggles are essential.

Tools for Applying Finish

There are a variety of tools on the market for applying finishes. The main types of tools are rags, brushes, and spray guns.

Rags and Cloths. Almost any type of clean cloth, preferably cotton, will work well for applying finishes. Listed below are some of the most common types.

- Old cotton T-shirt
- Paper Towels, especially useful for applying wiped-on finishes
- Tack Cloths, will last a week or two if stored in tightly capped containers, such as plastic peanut butter jars

Brushes. When choosing a brush, it's important to consider all of the features, especially bristle material and shape. Brush bristles are made of natural hair or synthetic fibers.

Natural hair brushes—oil-based finishes, laquers, varnishes, and shellacs.

Synthetic fiber brushes—water-based finishes and other non-oil-based finishes.

Brushes come in almost all shapes and sizes. Choose your shape and size according to your project needs.

Common types include **flat**, **angle**, **chisel**, **square**, and **round**. For example, you might choose a large, square brush for a project with large, flat areas. A smaller, rounded brush might help to reach detailed and hard-to-reach areas.

Spray Guns. Spray guns use compressed air to spray the finish onto your project. Using spray guns to apply finish can really save time, provided that the equipment fits into your budget. There are a variety of spray guns on the market, from the typical, mid-priced model to more transfer-efficient, high-priced models.

What Should I Use?

Which application method should you use for your project? This simple list should help:

- **Rags:** oils, oil/poly blends, and wiping poly stains
- **Brushes:** oil and water-based polyurethanes, brushing lacquers, stains
- **Spray guns:** lacquer

Your choice of application method will be partially driven by the result you have in mind. For example, the finish for a single piece of furniture can easily be wiped or brushed on, but if you have a stack of 25 kitchen cabinet doors to tackle, spraying will be much faster than the other approaches. It will also eliminate the risk of brushmarks and allow you to create the most uniform end product.

A note on spray guns: If you have a compressor, you can buy a spray gun that will work with it for a modest price. You can also purchase stand-alone HVLP (high volume, low pressure) sprayers that are easy to use and let you create pro-quality finishes pretty easily. Many of them are quite versatile, too—you can spray an outdoor fence or deck with the same tool that you'd use for fine furniture.

Finishing Tip: Popping the Grain

Popping wood grain emphasizes patterns. Coat with tung or linseed oil, let stand for 15 or 20 minutes, and wipe. Let dry. Apply a clear coat after waiting at least 12 hours. If you wish to add color, stain first.

Workbenches & Shop Set-Up

Every woodworker dreams of his or her own shop. At the heart of the shop is a good workbench. It's the starting point for moving on to more complex projects.

Workbenches

Whether you decide to purchase a workbench or build your own, the three major components you'll want to consider are space, utility, and cost. Choose a workbench that fits into the space you have available. Also consider any special features, such as vises or tops with different positions, that will aid you in the projects you create. If you decide to build your own workbench, there are a number of workbench plans available.

For beginners: A good beginning bench for woodworkers with little space is the Workmate® by Black & Decker. This small workbench is truly handy for a huge number of chores when a traditional workbench is not available.

For hand woodworking: European pattern workbenches are best. A hobby model will probably work well for most amateur woodworkers. Larger models can be heavy and expensive, but delightful to work on. Door and drawer kits help to customize these workbenches.

For carving: Specialty workbenches for carvers also exist, as well as handy clamp-on tables.

Workbench Ergonomics

Ergonomics is nothing more than the science of adapting conditions to make yourself comfortable while working. Each workbench must be the correct height for the user.

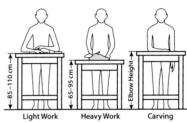

To measure for a hand tool workbench, start by holding a hand at your side, palm flat to the floor. Measure the distance. The distance you measured is the starter height for a hand tool woodworking bench.

Light Work 85 – 110 cm

Heavy Work 65 - 95 cm

Carving Elbow Height

For a power tool workbench, add at least 2" in height. As you adjust your workbench, remember that it is much easier to cut off an inch on each leg than it is to add an inch. If you're not sure of the exact height, start high and trim down.

Vises

There are a number of good woodworker's vises available. When checking for a new vise, look for features and capacity. Vises vary in size from 6" openings to about 12" openings.

Features include:
- **type of thread**
- **type of handle**
- **inclusion of a dog**
- **ease of changing liners**
  (wood or wood products to keep the vise from scratching your work)
- **ease of opening** (quick opening vises are exceptionally nice, but not essential)
- **overall quality**

Workbenches & Shop Set-Up

Sawhorses

Sawhorses are stands that are simple and inexpensive to make. They can also be purchased. Sawhorses have many uses, including holding wood for cutting and finishing. Combined with two 2x10s, sawhorses can make a workbench for hobbyists. A framing square makes layout easy.

Workshop Planning

The purpose of any woodworking shop is to have raw material come in one end and a finished product move out the other end. A small shop doesn't always need to be super-efficient, and a large one isn't automatically efficient. The shop may be small, but it works better if there is a distinct setting for each of the following operations:

- **Wood storage**
- **Working up rough wood**
- **Cutting to size**
- **Assembly**
- **Sanding and finishing**

Shop planning is easily done with graph paper and cut-outs of your most important tools. Start by outlining your space. Mark the electrical outlets. Make some scale or near scale flat cut-outs and move them around, checking to see what fits best and where. Note table heights on all power tools. In my shop, the small door is 48" wide by 8' tall, while the double door slides shut over an opening of more than 7' 6" width.

A common setup would begin with a **planer**, backed by a door, or double door, with the table saw next in line. Next to the **table saw** put the **jointer**. Then, set a **workbench** up for test assembly and hand woodworking. The **band saw** is close to the workbench, as is the **drill press**. If the band saw and drill press are on one side, a **lathe** can be placed on the other side, if desired. Set **major power tools** where workflow to and from them is efficient and safe. Decide on the areas of woodworking that interest you most and aim for a shop that suits those needs.

If you are finishing in a small shop, turn off all other operations, and let the dust settle for four hours or more. Arrange ventilation to clear fumes quickly.

A spark-free fan works best, but is expensive. Non-volatile finishes can be a good alternative. Be sure to use a good respirator, too.

Layout and Spacing

Keep in mind that each tool in your workshop needs its own specific type of layout and space. Laying out a shop and leaving the same size and shape of space for each tool reduces efficiency and safety and wastes a lot of area. Here are some common tools and their requirements:

- **Planer**—requires about 3' on at least three sides
- **Table saw**—requires space at one or both sides for cutting off long panels or boards
- **Jointer**—requires space in front and on both sides, can be placed against wall
- **Workbench**—requires space on front and on both sides (typically) depending on needs
- **Band saw**—requires about 5' in front and on both sides, can be placed against wall
- **Drill press**—requires about 3' in front and on both sides, can be placed against wall
- **Lathe**—requires about 3' in front, can be placed against wall

Floor Ergonomics

Working in a standing position on a regular basis can cause sore feet, swelling of the legs, varicose veins, general muscular fatigue, lower back pain, stiffness in the neck and shoulders, and other health problems. There are a few things that you can do to ease these problems.

- **Use Mats:** Mats placed on a concrete floor provide extra shock absorption and can ease discomfort and stiffness.
- **Get good footwear:** Quality footwear can give you the strength and stability needed for comfort.
- **Change your foot and body position:** Changing positions often will help to reduce muscle fatigue.
- **Use wood flooring instead of concrete:** Because wood flooring is softer than concrete flooring, wood is easier on your body.

CHAPTER 8

Shop Footwear Tips

- Wear shoes that do not change the shape of your foot.
- Choose shoes that give a firm grip for the heel. If the back of the shoe is too wide or too soft, the foot slips, causing instability and soreness.
- Wear shoes that give freedom to move your toes. If your shoes are too narrow or too shallow, your feet will hurt.
- Use shoes with arch supports.
- Wear shoes with laces.
- Tighten the laces firmly. Then, the foot won't slip inside the footwear.
- Pad under the tongue if there is tenderness in that area of the foot.
- Use shock-absorbing, cushioned insoles for working on cement floors.
- Do not wear flat shoes.
- Do not wear shoes with heels higher than two inches.
- Try on and walk in footwear before buying.

Lighting

Good lighting is essential for efficient and safe woodworking. As you plan for your shop, consider your natural and synthetic lighting needs. Each has its benefits and its drawbacks; an ideal workshop will often make use of both types of light.

Natural Lighting. Windows are great sources of natural light and ventilation, and work very well in finishing areas because of their ability to both give light and clear fumes. However, they can restrict tool placement by taking up wall space or because certain tools should not be positioned near glass.

Natural light changes from early morning through late evening, often throwing a glare in the windows that interferes with work. Sun position, clouds, and rainy weather all influence the light intensity and quality.

Synthetic Lighting. A shop properly lit with artificial lighting, can counteract the changes in the intensity, glare, and quality of natural light. Synthetic lights also allow you to position the light exactly where you need it. A spotlight, for example, can be very useful for lighting band saw or scroll saw blades as you cut.

Planning for Growth

Sooner or later, even a large shop has its walls hung with clamps, hand tools, templates, patterns, and much else. Make allowances for the increase in tools, jigs, templates, patterns, and other bits and pieces that come along.

Freestanding vs. Garage/Basement

With room to construct a freestanding shop, freedom of choice is a lot greater than if you have to use part of a basement. Here are some tips for both types of spaces.

Basement Shop

- **Headroom.** Try for as much headroom as possible. Swinging boards into place will be easier with more headroom.
- **Climate control.** Basements often include excess dampness. A dehumidifier helps, as can air conditioning in summer months.
- **Ventilation.** Basements often lack ventilation. Finishing outside or where there is better ventilation can be a good alternative.
- **Dust and noise problems.** Basement workshops can cause dust and noise problems for the rest of the house. Make certain that there is a good door between the shop and the furnace, with any air transfer going through filters. Do the same for any parts of the basement that are finished and not part of the shop—use good, tight fitting doors and keep them closed to keep the dust down.
- **Accessibility.** If the only door to a shop is a single door, it needs to be at least 42" wide to allow movement in and out of materials and projects. Having a basement shop can make it difficult to keep unauthorized people (especially kids) out of the shop area.

CHAPTER 8

Freestanding Shop

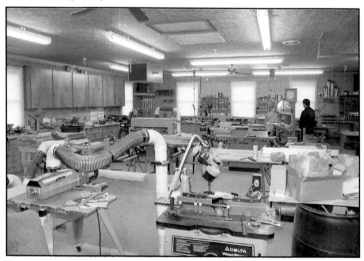

- **Headroom.** Because freestanding shops can be built to specifications, headroom is not as much of a problem as it can be in basement shops.
- **Climate control.** Wood moves with moisture, so it is helpful if a shop can be kept within reasonable humidity limits, similar to those in the average home (from 65°F to 75°F). Because both gluing operations and finishing operations work best at 60°F, temperature control is essential. If the temperature is too high, glues may not set properly and finishing will become difficult.
- **Ventilation.** Ventilation of finish odors is less of a problem in a freestanding shop, as this type of shop typically allows windows.
- **Dust and noise problems.** A good dust collection system is important in any type of shop, but it is probably needed more in a basement shop than in a well-ventilated free-standing shop. Wear a mask!
- **Accessibility.** Be sure to have a door that is at least 42" wide to allow movement in and out of materials and projects. Freestanding shops may use overhead garage doors. The new openers are a welcome addition.

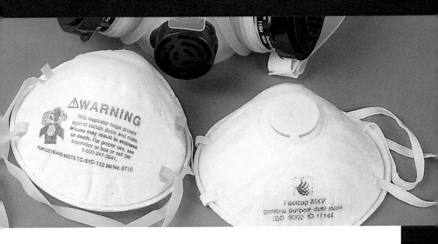

CHAPTER 9

Safety in the Woodshop

Safety starts with mental processes. Woodworking can be a dangerous recreation or business, and no amount of safety gear or advice can replace thinking safe. Think about a process first. If it seems unsafe, find another way to do the work. Know what tools are the most dangerous, know what kickback areas and distances are, know where to stand when starting any powered tool, and know to keep your hands and fingers away from the sharp spinning bits and blades. If you know these things, you'll soon work out new ways to increase your safety.

First Aid Kits

Install a good first aid kit at a spot easily reached in the shop. If you are putting your own kit together, place all contents in a container that is easy to recognize. Marking it with a red cross or large red letters that say "First Aid" helps anyone not familiar with your shop.

Suggested contents:

- alcohol wipes
- sterilizing solution for cuts (i.e., providone-iodine solution, commonly called Betadine)
- band-aids
- small compresses (sterile gauze)
- a good pair of tweezers and a magnifying glass for removing splinters
- needles for splinter removal stored in a small jar of alcohol
- rubber gloves for dealing with severe bleeding injuries to other people or for other people to work with your injuries
- burn lotion
- aspirin or acetaminophen
- eyewash, an eyecup, and a small hand mirror for eye inspections
- non-prescription allergy medication for reactions with wood
- an extra of any necessary prescriptions (i.e., an inhaler for those with asthma)

Breathing Protection

There are dozens of different masks and respirators to take care of the job.

Masks

Masks keep sanding dust from your lungs. A dust mask does fine for wood and plastic cutting operations, and may not even be needed if dust collection systems are efficient. For sanding operations, a dust mask is a good idea, even with a good dust collection system.

Safety in the Woodshop

Fit and comfort are important with all masks. The cartridge styles often come in several face sizes (small, medium, large) and are made with molded rubber to closely fit the face. Full beards create interference with the fit of all masks, except the full-coverage, powered type.

Respirators

Respirators filter out VOCs (volatile organic compounds) and have cartridges, with single or dual exchangeable filters, just below the eyesight line of the mask. Organic vapor cartridges are needed for most woodworking finishing applications to keep fumes from lacquer and varnish out of your lungs and to stop the effects of other sprays, such as laminate (contact) adhesives.

If you work frequently with exotic wood, you may be exposed to a wide variety of allergens that weren't around years ago. Thus, when a lot of shavings of, for example, rosewood are going to be curling up or flying around, it's a sensible step to keep every bit out of your lungs, out of your eyes, and off the rest of your body. Battery powered respirators are excellent for any situation where heavy dust is a problem, whether it is wood dust, plaster sanding dust, fiberglass dust, or some similar compound.

- **Filters.** Some respirators have filters that can remove almost anything in a woodshop. Up to 99.97% effective, they work to filter out dust, particulates, paint spray, organic vapors, acid vapors, and asbestos dust. Different cartridges can filter out fewer of these—for instance, one type could filter all six; another type could filter the first four (dust, particulates, paint spray, and organic vapors) but not all six.
- **Using a Battery-Powered Respirator.** If you're doing hazardous heavy duty work, or working a lathe, try the newer battery powered respirators. They give almost all-in-one coverage. These respirators protect the eyes with a shield, the ears with muffs, and the lungs with powered air drawn through both a prefilter and a cartridge.

Safety in the Woodshop

CHAPTER 9

Hearing Protection

Hearing protection is easy, cheap, and comes in two main forms: earplugs and earmuffs.

Earplugs

Foam earplugs offer just about the cheapest and best ear protection available. Beeswax earplugs do not offer sufficient protection and are not comparable to foam plugs. Select ones that feel comfortable in your ears. Consider buying about five pairs of earplugs if you share your shop or if you often have guests. You might consider keeping a container of foam earplugs, the straight and inexpensive kind that works very well, at or near the entrance. Hand them out if there will be any machinery running, because noise limits are lower than we'd like to believe.

Common varieties of earplugs:

- plain foam
- shaped foam
- one-time wear
- reusable
- earplugs with cords
- earplugs with headsets

Earmuffs

Plain old mute muffs can reduce decibel count very well, but the seals around the muffs lose their effectiveness over time and need replacing. Some earmuffs allow you to listen to music. Electronic earmuffs reduce sound, but allow low-level sounds to come through electronically. Choose earmuffs that are comfortable to wear and adjust easily.

Most earmuffs offer protection around 30 dB, and most don't seal perfectly after a time, so that level drops. For the greatest sound protection, some people recommend using earplugs inside earmuffs, but that over-protection may mask some harsh sounds that could prove helpful to safety.

Levels of Common Sounds	
140	Painful, gunshot
135	Jet plane take off, over-amped music
120	Chainsaw
90	OSHA limit, extended exposure here and above causes hearing damage
60a	Normal conversation
45	Soft music
30	whisper

Occupational Safety and Health Administration Cumulative Safe Noise Exposure Times	
Maximum Cumulative Exposure Time Per Day	Sound Level (dBA)
8 hours	90 and down
4 hours	95
2 hours	100
1 hour	105
Half-an-hour	110
Quarter-hour or under	115
Avoid entirely	Over 115

CHAPTER 9

Eye Protection

Shop eye protection includes glasses bought as safety glasses, which have high impact polycarbonate lenses, to sunglass style glasses to goggles meant for high impact use to face shields rated for resistance to impact. The particular rating needed is ANSI Z87.1.

General guidelines for eye protection:

■ Always use glasses that have a wraparound or mountable side shields, no matter what other features they have. Chips and dust have a tendency to hit from the side even when you think they are coming head-on.

■ Face shields should be selected for fast adjustability of headband (if more than one person is going to use them), ease of lifting the shield up and out of the way for close checks of the work, and ease of replacement of the shield itself when it becomes battered and scarred.

■ Nothing will protect you from large flying chunks, short of a suit of armor. To protect your face, you need a low-dust condition because a standard face shield does not work well with a dust mask or respirator. To handle large flying chunks, make sure you're out of the line of fire after you have made sure that everything is as well-adjusted as possible and that there are no problems with your tools.

Safety Feature

The foundation of the SawStop is a replaceable cartridge. The SawStop's sensors inductively feel contact with flesh and drop the cartridge out, resulting in the blade losing contact with flesh, in about five milliseconds. The cartridge is ruined, of course, as is the saw blade, but considering the fact that the saw user retains a finger, hand, or other body part, and gets no more than a nick in most cases, that's cheap.

Mountable Safety Items

Mountable safety items are primarily aimed at the table saw, though splitters also work with shapers.

Overarm Blade Guards

The optional overarm (cantilever) blade guard is available from a number of makers. This guard offers more protection than the stock blade guard and is easier to remove.

The system looks simple on first glance: a box-like polycarbonate guard is suspended on the arm or parallelogram and adjusts up and down by a crank or by rod and knob. Counterbalancing eases the movement for those with arms, or parallelograms; a knob locks the setting. A longer arm extends to one side or the back of the table, and any dust collection hose or tube goes along with it.

The upper arm is adjustable for width, and the box can be raised and lowered easily over the blade. The box and its hold-downs detach quickly for times when it will interfere with cutting. Dismounting and remounting of any of the guards takes seconds and no tools. Many brands can be adapted for other mounting styles (i.e., a ceiling mount version).

Splitters

Several of the overarm blade guards come with splitters. Most are designed for cabinet saws. Overall, first installation takes a little time, and, on some saws, might require drilling a hole or two. Once installed and adjusted, splitters are lift off devices, unlike the stock splitter that must be unbolted or unscrewed every time it's removed.

CHAPTER 9

Stock Feeder
This safety device is useful on both tablesaws and shapers. A simple, correctly mounted stock feeder—sized to the power of its tool—can improve cuts a tremendous amount, while almost eliminating any chance of kickback from either the shaper or the table saw. Once the feeder is set, there is no need for your hands to be even within a couple of feet of any sharp, spinning bits, adding even more to your safety.

Feather Boards
Feather boards provide much of the same protection that a stock feeder does, at much lower cost. They have flexible "fingers" and are used to feed wood through the tablesaw or shaper. Feather boards can be mounted with magnets, clamped on, slotted into miter slots, or locked in place numerous other ways.

Other Safety Items
Safety is a constant need in the woodshop, and it doesn't always involve possible loss of body parts, vision, or the ability to breathe.

Kneepads
Being able to stand up without knee pain after a day of installing and leveling base cabinets can be a large help, aided by kneepads. Gel kneepads work nicely, with a softer cap that keeps you from slipping—something very handy on tile floors— and a slick-capped version that makes turning and pivoting to locate and pick up the next bolt much easier.

Gloves
Work gloves are a good way to protect your hands. For overall rough work—feeding a planer or stacking lumber, for instance—gloves that enclose the entire hand work a little bit better. Other gloves leave the thumb and forefinger open for gripping when excellent control is needed. While gloves are often considered comfort items rather than safety items, they're worth thought because a comfortable worker is a safer worker.

of a square · length x width
of a rectangle · · · · · · · · · · · · · · · · · · · 1/2 x base x height
a of a triangle · base x height
a of a parallelogram · · · · · · · · · · · · · · height x 1/2(a + b + c + d)
ea of a trapezoid · · · · · · · · · 3.141592, etc. or approximately 22/7
(π) · · · · · · · · · · · 3.141592, etc. or approximately · · · π x d or 2πr
ircumference of a circle · C/π
Diameter of a circle · C/2
Radius of a circle · πr2
Area of a circle · (ø/360) x πr2
of a sector of a circle · · · · · · · · · · · · · · · 120 x F/
· · · · · · F x

CHAPTER 10

Common Formulas & Shop Math

Charts and formulas can help when you're working wood, but it is a good idea to test all initial cuts in same-size scrap wood before cutting into more costly materials.

Quick reference for formulas

Area of a square......... length x width

Area of a rectangle ..... length x width

Area of a triangle .....½ x base x height

Area of a parallelogram ...base x height

Area of a trapezoid ....
height x ½(a + b + c + d)

Pi (π) ....3.141592, etc. or approx. $^{22}/_{7}$

Circumference of a circle ....π x d or 2πr

Diameter of a circle .... C/π

Radius of a circle C/2π

Area of a circle .... $πr^2$

Area of a sector of a circle ....
½ x arc length x r

Motor speed.................. 120 x F/P

Work .... F x D

Torque............................ F x D

Full-load torque .... hp x 5252/rpm

Horsepower ....
V x I x Eff/746 or T x rpm/5252

Board feet ....(T x W x L)/144

CHAPTER 10

Circles, Ellipses, & Arches

Circles are the simplest of the three. To draw a circle, you need a center and a radius or a diameter. To find the distance around a circle, use pi (π) x d (the diameter) or 2πr (radius). To determine the area, use πr2. If you need to find the area of a sphere, the area is four times the area of the circle the sphere is based on.

Ellipses are a bit harder to draw than circles; however, the ellipses used for most woodworking projects do not have to be highly accurate. They're used frequently, so mastering one of the accepted methods to figure size and to draw an ellipse is a handy skill. Ellipses show up as arches in project molding or similar decorative touches. Remember: an ellipse is not an oval—an ellipse is symmetrical; an oval is not.

Drawing an ellipse

The method given here is a simple way to draw an ellipse that is accurate for most woodworking needs.

1. Start with a rectangle that is the same size as the ellipse you wish to make. As the drawing shows, the long axis is called the major axis. The short axis is called the minor axis. Mark the axes on the paper.
2. Use a divider set at half the length of the major axis. Swing an arc starting at the top of the minor axis (point C), so that the arc crosses the major axis at two points (points E and F).
3. Place small nails at those crossing points (E and F) and at the top of the minor axis (point C). Tie a loop of string around the points.
4. Pull the nail at the top of the minor axis, hold a pencil on the string, and slowly draw your ellipse.

Ellipse

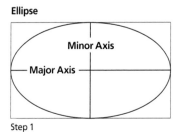

Minor Axis

Major Axis

Step 1

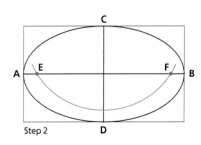

Step 2

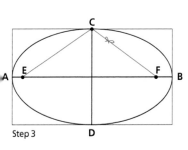

Step 3

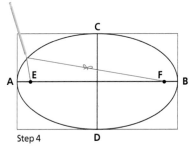

Step 4

CHAPTER 10

Arches are ever present in woodworking and are easy to lay out if there is a specified radius. You'll need the chord length and the rise of the arch to make a trammel that will let you lay out the correct arch. Start by drawing a line the width of the chord. Mark the center and measure the rise. Set a trammel and draw a circle around the rise mark. Next, draw circles around each end of the chord. Where the lines meet on the resulting three circles, draw lines straight through. Where those two lines meet, place the trammel, after setting it to the arc radius, and draw the arc.

Right Angles

To square up a corner, choose a point in the corner and measure 3 x 4 x 5 units. One leg is 3, one leg is 4, and the hypotenuse is 5. No matter what units you prefer—inches, feet, yards, meters—the corner will be square if your measurements are accurate. Any multiple of these numbers will work, such as 6' x 8' x 10' or 1½" x 2" x 2½".

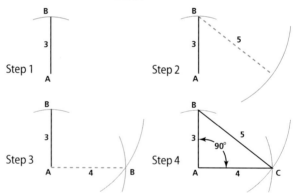

Quick Measurement Conversions

144 square inches	1 square foot
1728 cubic inches	1 cubic foot
9 square feet	1 square yard
27 cubic feet	1 cubic yard
30¼ yards	1 square rod
640 acres	1 square mile

Conversion Chart

The English System of Measurement to the Metric System

To convert from (English):	To (Metric):	Multiply English measurement by
Acre (a)	Square meter (m²)	4,046.8564
Acre (a)	Hectare (ha)	0.4047
Square foot (ft²)	Square meter (m²)	0.0929
Square inch (in²)	Square meter (m²)	0.00064516
Square mile (mi²)	Square meter (m²)	2,589,988.1
Square yard (yd²)	Square meter (m²)	.8361
Fathom (fath)	Meter (m)	1.8288
Foot (ft)	Meter (m)	0.3048
Inch (in)	Centimeter (cm)	2.54
Inch (in)	Millimeter (mm)	25.4
Mile (mi)	Meter (m)	1,609.344
Mile (mi)	Kilometer (km)	1.609344
Mile, nautical	Kilometer (km)	1.852
Point (computer, 1/72 in)	Millimeter (mm)	0.3527777
Rod (rd)	Meter (m)	5.0292
Yard (yd)	Meter (m)	0.9144

Crown Molding Angles

Crown molding may be cut-tipped to the fence. When you're using this method, no bevel cut is needed, and adjustments for out-of-square corners are fast and easy.

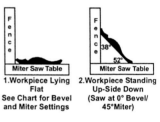

1. Workpiece Lying Flat
See Chart for Bevel and Miter Settings

2. Workpiece Standing Up-Side Down
(Saw at 0° Bevel/ 45° Miter)

Build a support jig for best results. The jig shown is simple; it should be built to custom-fit the height of the molding tilted against the fence face. The fence temporarily mounts on the standard slide compound miter saw fence, through holes that are already in the saw fence. Wood should be well-prepared hardwood, such as maple, birch, or white oak, ½" thick. Length depends on the miter saw you're using—full width of the saw fence is best. Make sure you don't place any

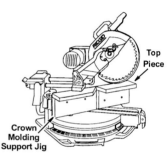

Top Piece

Crown Molding Support Jig

nails or screws in the direct cut line. You'll need a fence for each corner angle you'll be cutting. Fences take only five minutes to make, and even with four corners, it's worth the time.

If you don't work with molding daily, spatial relationships are often hard to visualize. Always make and test each cut in scrap before making the final cuts in good stock. Remember, when the molding is standing up, you do not need to make a bevel cut.

Wall to Crown Molding Angle: 45 degrees

Wall Angle (deg.)	Bevel Angle (deg.)	Miter Angle (deg.)	Wall Angle (deg.)	Bevel Angle (deg.)	Miter Angle (deg.)	Wall Angle (deg.)	Bevel Angle (deg.)	Miter Angle (deg.)
60	37.8	50.8	86	31.1	37.2	112	23.3	25.5
61	37.5	50.2	87	30.9	36.7	113	23.0	25.1
62	37.3	49.6	88	30.6	36.2	114	22.7	24.7
63	37.1	49.1	89	30.3	35.7	115	22.3	24.3
64	36.8	48.5	90	30.0	35.3	116	22.0	23.8
65	36.6	48.0	91	29.7	34.8	117	21.7	23.4
66	36.4	47.4	92	29.4	34.3	118	21.4	23.0
67	36.1	46.9	93	29.1	33.9	119	21.0	22.6
68	35.9	46.4	94	28.8	33.4	120	20.7	22.2
69	35.6	45.8	95	28.5	32.9	121	20.4	21.8
70	35.4	45.3	96	28.2	32.5	122	20.0	21.4
71	35.1	44.8	97	27.9	32.0	123	19.7	21.0
72	34.9	44.2	98	27.6	31.6	124	19.4	20.6
73	34.6	43.7	99	27.3	31.1	125	19.1	20.2
74	34.4	43.2	100	27.0	30.7	126	18.7	19.8
75	34.1	42.7	101	26.7	30.2	127	18.4	19.4
76	33.9	42.1	102	26.4	29.8	128	18.1	19.0
77	33.6	41.6	103	26.1	29.4	129	17.7	18.6
78	33.3	41.1	104	25.8	28.9	130	17.4	18.2
79	33.1	40.6	105	25.5	28.5	131	17.1	17.9
80	32.8	40.1	106	25.2	28.1	132	16.7	17.5
81	32.5	39.6	107	24.9	27.6	133	16.4	17.1
82	32.3	39.1	108	24.6	27.2	134	16.0	16.7
83	32.0	38.6	109	24.2	26.8	135	15.7	16.3
84	31.7	38.1	110	23.9	26.3	136	15.4	15.9
85	31.4	37.7	111	23.6	25.9	137	15.0	15.6

COURTESY RIDGID

Continued on next page

Common Formulas & Shop Math

CHAPTER 10

Wall to Crown Molding Angle: 45 degrees, continued

Ceiling

Wall

Wall Angle (deg.)	Bevel Angle (deg.)	Miter Angle (deg.)	Wall Angle (deg.)	Bevel Angle (deg.)	Miter Angle (deg.)	Wall Angle (deg.)	Bevel Angle (deg.)	Miter Angle (deg.)
138	14.7	15.2	153	9.5	9.6	168	4.2	4.3
139	14.3	14.8	154	9.2	9.3	169	3.9	3.9
140	14.0	14.4	155	8.8	8.9	170	3.5	3.5
141	13.7	14.1	156	8.5	8.5	171	3.2	3.2
142	13.3	13.7	157	8.1	8.2	172	2.8	2.8
143	13.0	13.3	158	7.8	7.8	173	2.5	2.5
144	12.6	12.9	159	7.4	7.5	174	2.1	2.1
145	12.3	12.6	160	7.1	7.1	175	1.8	1.8
146	11.9	12.2	161	6.7	6.7	176	1.4	1.4
147	11.6	11.8	162	6.4	6.4	177	1.1	1.1
148	11.2	11.5	163	6.0	6.0	178	0.7	0.7
149	10.9	11.1	164	5.6	5.7	179	0.4	0.4
150	10.5	10.7	165	5.3	5.3	180	0.0	0.0
151	10.2	10.4	166	4.9	5.0			
152	9.8	10.0	167	4.6	4.6			

Common Formulas & Shop Math

Wall to Crown Molding Angle: 52/38 degrees

Wall Angle (deg.)	Bevel Angle (deg.)	Miter Angle (deg.)	Wall Angle (deg.)	Bevel Angle (deg.)	Miter Angle (deg.)	Wall Angle (deg.)	Bevel Angle (deg.)	Miter Angle (deg.)
△ 60	43.0	46.8	86	35.2	33.4	112	26.1	22.6
61	42.8	46.3	87	34.9	33.0	113	25.8	22.2
62	42.5	45.7	88	34.5	32.5	114	25.4	21.8
63	42.2	45.1	89	34.2	32.1	115	25.0	21.4
64	41.9	44.6	⌐ 90	33.9	31.6	116	24.7	21.0
65	41.7	44.0	91	33.5	31.2	117	24.3	20.7
66	41.4	43.5	92	33.2	30.7	118	23.9	20.3
67	41.1	42.9	93	32.8	30.3	119	23.6	19.9
68	40.8	42.4	94	32.5	29.9	⌐ 120	23.2	19.6
69	40.5	41.9	95	32.2	29.4	121	22.8	19.2
70	40.2	41.3	96	31.8	29.0	122	22.5	18.8
71	39.9	40.8	97	31.5	28.6	123	22.1	18.5
72	39.6	40.3	98	31.1	28.2	124	21.7	18.1
73	39.3	39.2	99	30.8	27.7	125	21.3	17.8
74	39.0	39.2	100	30.4	27.3	126	21.0	17.4
75	38.7	38.7	101	30.1	26.9	127	20.6	17.1
76	38.4	38.2	102	29.7	26.5	128	20.2	16.7
77	38.1	37.7	103	29.4	26.1	129	19.8	16.4
78	37.8	37.2	104	29.0	25.7	130	19.5	16.0
79	37.4	36.8	105	28.7	25.3	131	19.1	15.7
80	37.1	36.3	106	28.3	24.9	132	18.7	15.3
81	36.8	35.8	107	28.0	24.5	133	18.3	15.0
82	36.5	35.3	108	27.6	24.1	134	17.9	14.6
83	36.2	34.8	109	27.2	23.7	135	17.6	14.3
84	35.8	34.4	110	26.9	23.3	136	17.2	14.0
85	35.5	33.9	111	26.5	22.9	137	16.8	13.6

Continued on next page

Common Formulas & Shop Math

Wall to Crown Molding Angle: $^{52}/_{38}$ degrees, continued

Ceiling 52°
Wall 38°

Wall Angle (deg.)	Bevel Angle (deg.)	Miter Angle (deg.)	Wall Angle (deg.)	Bevel Angle (deg.)	Miter Angle (deg.)	Wall Angle (deg.)	Bevel Angle (deg.)	Miter Angle (deg.)
138	16.4	13.3	153	10.8	8.4	168	4.7	3.7
139	16.0	13.0	154	10.2	8.1	169	4.3	3.4
140	15.6	12.8	155	9.8	7.8	170	3.9	3.1
141	15.3	12.3	156	9.4	7.5	171	3.5	2.8
142	14.9	12.0	157	9.0	7.1	172	3.2	2.5
143	14.5	11.6	158	8.6	6.8	173	2.8	2.2
144	14.1	11.3	159	8.3	6.5	174	2.4	1.8
145	13.7	11.0	160	7.9	6.2	175	2.0	1.5
146	13.3	10.7	161	7.5	5.9	176	1.6	1.2
147	12.9	10.3	162	7.1	5.6	177	1.2	0.9
148	12.5	10.0	163	6.7	5.3	178	0.8	0.6
149	12.2	9.7	164	6.3	4.9	179	0.4	0.3
150	11.8	9.4	165	5.9	4.6	180	0.0	0.0
151	11.4	9.0	166	5.5	4.3			
152	11.0	8.7	167	5.1	4.0			

COURTESY RIDGID

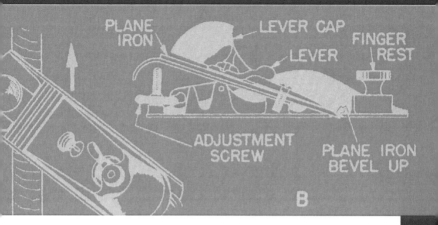

PLANE IRON

PLANE IRON

LEVER CAP

LEVER

FINGER REST

ADJUSTMENT SCREW

PLANE IRON BEVEL UP

B

Glossary & Index

Glossary

Air-dried: Method of seasoning lumber without using power or extra heat. Wood is stacked (stickered between rows) and the top covered. The wood is then left to season, allowing one year for every 1" of thickness.

Aluminum Oxide: Man-made abrasive material based on aluminum ore (bauxite). Fused with silica and iron. Harder than garnet. Grayish brown color.

Annual Growth Rings: Layer of wood grown during a single growing season. Temperate Zone annual growth rings of many species (e.g., oaks, and pines) are readily distinguished because of differences in the cells formed during the early and late parts of the season. In some Temperate Zone species (black gum and sweetgum) and many tropical species, annual growth rings are not easily recognized.

Apron: The part of a table just under the top. May or may not contain drawers.

Apron Plane: Small plane that fits easily in a shop apron pocket.

Arbor: Revolving spindle of a table saw or other tool.

ATB: Configuration of teeth on a circular saw blade, alternate top bevel. Usually for crosscutting.

Auger: Hand-drilling tool with a fairly long twist to the flutes. Referred to as an auger bit when used with a bit brace.

Awl: Marking tool for woodworking. Also useful for starting small nails, screws. May be round or square shanked, long or short bladed.

Back Board (Backer Board): Usually scrap, piece used to prevent reverse side tear-out when making cuts with router bits, saw blades, other edged tools.

Back Saw: Any of several saws with a strengthening spine on the upper back edge.

Banding (Inlay): Thin strips in patterns, usually 2" down to as little as ⅛" wide, seldom more than ¹⁄₁₆" thick.

Beeswax: A soft, mildly sticky form of wax from honeybees. Used for making wax polish. Also used to lubricate screws, wood slides, similar fittings.

Bench Dog: A metal or wood peg, with spring, that fits into a line of round or square holes in the workbench top, forming end stops for pieces being cut, sanded, or otherwise worked on.

Bench Holdfast: Device that fits in dog holes to hold pieces flat on bench surface.

Bench Planes: Smoothing, jack, and try planes. Also panel planes, though those are even less frequently used today. These are called bench planes because in the past they spent most of their time on the bench, ready to be used.

Bevel: An edge at any angle other than 90°, basically a sloped or canted surface. Also, filing angle for saw teeth.

Bevel-Edge Chisel: A chisel with the long edges beveled to help ease waste removal.

Bird's Eye: Small areas in wood with the fibers indented and otherwise contorted to form small circular or elliptical figures resembling birds' eyes on the tangential surface. Found in sugar maple; rare in other hardwood species; decorative.

Block Plane: A small plane, usually metal, for trimming small work and end grain. Regular pitch is about 20°. Low angle block planes have irons (cutters or blades) at 12°.

Board Foot: A board 12" long, 12" wide, and 1" thick or its equivalent. In practice, the board foot calculation for lumber 1" or more in thickness is based on its nominal thickness and width and the actual length. Lumber with a nominal thickness of less than 1" is calculated as 1".

Bow: The distortion of lumber in which there is deviation from the flat face, from a straight line end-to- end of the piece.

Bullnose Plane: A small plane, usually metal, that looks like a shoulder plane, with a nose shortened to ease working close into corners, stopped rabbets, and similar positions.

Burl: (1) Hard, woody outgrowth on a tree, more or less rounded in form, resulting from the entwined growth of a cluster of buds. The source of highly figured burl veneers used ornamentally. (2) In lumber or veneer, a localized severe distortion of the grain generally rounded in outline, resulting from overgrowth of dead branch stubs, varying from ½" to several inches in diameter.

Burnisher: Tool for turning a wire edge on a sharpened cabinet scraper.

Burr: (1) Wire edge formed when sharpening some cutters; (2) A special figuring in some wood, much like a lot of small knots packed in tightly together.

Butt Joint: A joint whereby parts are merely cut square to each other.

Button: Device for joining tabletops to aprons or cabinet frames.

Calipers: Gauges for measuring inside or outside diameters or lengths.

Cam: Irregular curved lobe on a rotating shaft to give spaced motion.

Cam Clamps: A clamp with a deep throat designed to provide fairly gentle clamping pressure. Pressure is applied by moving a cam that locks the lower jaw in place. Very useful to luthiers.

Cam-Out: A common problem in drilling where the driver tip moves off the screw head when power is applied.

Cannel: The angle of the bevel on a gouge or chisel. Outside bevels are "out-cannels" while inside bevels are "in-cannels."

Cant: A slant as in a bevel or tilt. Also, the long, spiked-end tool for turning logs.

Carcass (UK spelling is Carcase): Skeleton of furniture or cabinets before doors, drawers, or other parts are fitted.

Carnauba Wax: A very hard vegetable wax often added to beeswax to make a polish wax with some of the traits of each.

Carver's Burs: Cutters that are attached to a flexible shaft driven by a motor. May be steel (high speed steel) or carbide.

Carver's Chisel: Widely varying shapes in cutting tools used by carvers.

Center Bit: A bit with a center point, often a spur point, sometimes a screw threaded spur point.

Centers: Pivots for lathes, one in the tail stock and one in the head stock. Live centers revolve with the wood to reduce friction.

Chalking: Becoming powdery or chalky; reaction of some adhesives when set at an improper temperature.

Chamfer: An angle planed on an edge. Lightens appearance, may help reduce splintering. Similar to a bevel, but usually not as wide.

Chatoyance: Tendency towards iridescence. Lustrous.

GLOSSARY & INDEX

Check: A lengthwise separation of the wood that usually extends across the rings of annual growth, caused by stresses set up in wood during seasoning.

Chord: A line segment that joins any two points on an arc, curve, or circle.

Chuck: A device to hold a bit or cutter in braces, drills, lathes.

Circular Saw: Any saw that uses a circular blade. In the U.S., circular saws include handheld—both corded and cordless—table saws, and circular saws in sawmills. Tooth types are designed to do specific jobs from ripping wood to crosscutting, and to handle different materials, including woods, manufactured woods, plastics, and non-ferrous metals.

Close-Grained Wood: Wood with narrow annual rings. Wood with small, closely spaced pores. Fine-textured.

Coarse-Grained Wood: Wood with wide annual rings, considerable difference between springwood and summerwood. Wood with large pores, such as oak, ash, chestnut, and walnut. Coarse-textured.

Collet: A type of chuck on a router that holds the bit in place.

Combination Oilstone: Coarse oilstone on one side, fine on the other.

Conditioning: Exposing material to a prescribed atmosphere for a stated period of time or until a specific relation is reached between material and atmosphere.

Coniferous: Cone-bearing trees. Usually classed as softwoods.

Contact Adhesive (or Cement): Adhesive for laminates, with parts assembled after the cement coats both sides and is nearly dry. Long-lasting, but not really permanent.

Coopering: Building up cylindrical surfaces.

Coped Joint: A joint that is cut in molding in the shape of the molding pattern, often after the molding is mitered or otherwise cut at an angle.

Coping Saw: A saw with the blade held in tension in a metal frame. Cuts shapes in thin wood. Usually turning the handle tightens the blade.

Core: The core is the structure of the internal filler of plywoods, and includes lumber, MDF, and plywoods.

Corner Chisel: Chisel designed to cut a square corner.

Counterboring: Drilling a hole that recesses a screwhead deeply into the wood. Allows use of a shorter screw, but also allows covering the screw with a dowel plug.

Countersink: A bit used to recess a screwhead flush with the surface.

Crosscut: Cutting across the grain.

Crosscut Saw: A saw designed to cut across the grain of the wood.

Cure Time: The length of time it takes an adhesive to become fully dried so that it can be put into full-time use.

Curly-Grained Wood: Wood with fibers distorted so that they have a curled appearance, as in bird's eye wood.

Cutterhead: The part of a jointer or planer that holds the blades and turns with them.

Cylinder: A geometric shape of uniform circular section.

Dado: A groove cut across the grain of wood.

Deciduous: Leaf dropping trees, for the most part, in temperate zones. Usually classed as hardwoods.

Density: Density is the mass of wood substance enclosed within a unit volume. It is variously expressed as pounds per cubic foot, kilograms per cubic meter, or grams per cubic centimeter at specified moisture content.

Depth Gauge: Device fitted to a bit or drill to indicate when a particular depth has been reached.

Depth Stop: Device that prevents a bit or auger from going deeper than a set depth.

Double-Faced Tape: Tape with adhesive on both sides, useful for lathe work, holding patterns and templates in place.

Dovetail Saw: A small back saw with a short blade, fine teeth. Japanese dovetail saws have even finer teeth.

Dowel Center: Markers that fit into drilled holes to transfer dowel center markings for accurate dowel placement.

Dowel Plate: Used for producing dowels by hand. A sized piece of wood is driven through the appropriately sized hole.

Dowel Screw: Double ended (different threads) screw, with a blank center to allow turning.

Dowelling Jig: A jig that allows accurate boring of pairs of holes for dowels.

Draw Boring: Using a pin to draw a tenon more tightly into a mortise.

Dress: To shape a grinding wheel, uncovering fresh abrasive and flattening the wheel.

Dressed Size: Dimensions of lumber after being surfaced with a planing machine. Dressed size is usually ½" to ¾" less than nominal or rough size. A 2" x 4" stud, for example, actually measures about 1½" x 3½".

Durability: The ability of a wood to resist rot and insect damage.

Dust Collector: Tool used to collect dust directly from powered machines, usually has bags for collection.

Dye: Type of wood stain, usually aniline or spirit.

Edge-Grained Lumber: Lumber sawed so that the wide surfaces extend approximately at right angles to the annual growth rings. Lumber is considered edge-grained when the rings form an angle of 45° to 90° with the wide surface of the piece. Quarter-sawn.

Ellipse: Cross section of a cone or cylinder at any angle other than a right angle to the axis.

End Check: A split in a board end occurring during the seasoning process.

End Grain: Grain exposed by a cross cut at an approximate right angle to the grain length.

Epoxy Resin: Adhesive, thermo-setting, synthetic, two-part adhesive that can be designed to have long working times, short working times, and cure in cold temperatures, and can be mixed to fill small and large gaps.

Equilibrium Moisture Content: Moisture content at which wood neither gains nor loses moisture when surrounded by air at a given relative humidity and temperature.

Equilateral Triangle: Triangle with all three sides equal, all three angles 60°.

Face: The "top" of a piece of wood, the most visible area after work is finished.

Face Measure: The area in square feet or inches of a board's surface.

Faceplate: Metal plate attached to a lathe mandrel in place of a chuck. Has screw holes that flat items may be fixed to. Used for turning plates and bowls.

Facing: Edging, or thin strip of hardwood glued to another type of board.

Featherboards (Fingerboards): Boards cut with lightweight fingers (feathers) that are set to press against work to hold it safely in place.

Fence: Metal, wood, or plastic faced guides for tools that keep the workpiece feeding straight, or keep the tool straight on the workpiece.

Fiddleback-Grained Wood: Figure of a fine wavy grain found in a species of maple; traditionally used for the backs of violins.

Figure: Loose term used for the decorative appearance of wood. It may include various less-than-usual types such as bird's eye, curly, fiddle, and others.

Flap Sander: A narrow drum with flaps of sandpaper fixed around its perimeter. Usually driven by a power drill, some also are mounted on stationary machines. Effective for sanding irregular surfaces.

Flat-Grained Wood: Lumber sawed parallel to the pith and tangent to the growth rings. Lumber is flat-grained when the annual growth rings make an angle of less than 45° with the surface of the piece. Flat or plain-sawn.

Flat-Sawn: Lumber cut at a tangent through the annual rings. Also called plain-sawn.

Forstner Bit: A bit guided by its circular rim instead of a spur or point.

Fretsaw: Similar to a coping saw, but made to use finer blades; may also have a clearance between frame and blade of 16" or more.

FTG: Flat tooth grind. Configuration of tip grind on a circular saw blade, usually for rip blades.

Frog: Sloping bed against which a plane cutter rests. In metal planes, it is most often adjustable.

Gap-filling Adhesive: An adhesive suitable for bonding surfaces where joints are at least .05" apart. Epoxy is the most notable gap filling adhesive, and the strongest.

Glue Blocks: Blocks glued into corners to add gluing surface, thus strengthening the joint.

Grain: The direction, size, arrangement, appearance, or quality of the fibers in wood or lumber.

Grain Filler: Silica or other powder added to carrier (often shellac in a very thin cut) to fill pores on ring porous woods.

Green Wood: Freshly sawn or undried wood.

Gum: A comprehensive term for nonvolatile viscous plant exudates, which either dissolve or swell up in contact with water.

Hardwoods: Trees with broad leaves. The term has little real reference to the hardness of the wood—balsa is a hardwood, for example.

Haunch: Slight projection at the side of a tenon. Helps resist twisting.

Heartwood: Wood extending from the pith to the sapwood, the cells of which no longer participate in the life processes of the tree. Heartwood contains gums, resins, and other materials that make it darker than sapwood.

Heel: The wide end of a skew chisel or saw tooth.

Hold Fast: A device that enables wood to be held down firmly on the bench.

Hollow Chisel: Chisel used on a hollow chisel mortiser. It is hollow to accept a drill bit that removes the major part of the waste in the mortise being cut.

Honing: Finishing an edge on the oilstone after a tool has been ground. May also be used to mean-hone on leather, though that is often called stropping.

Horsepower: Unit of power measurement. 1 HP=33,000 ft.lbs. of work per minute. The electrical equivalent is 746 watts for a single horsepower.

Hot-Melt Adhesives: Thermoplastic adhesives that are heated so that they spread easily and cool rapidly.

Housed Joint: Any joint in which one part is recessed into another. (i.e., housed dado)

HSS: High speed steel. Steel used for saw blades and other cutting tools. For power tools, tungsten carbide has just about taken its place, but it is still found in hand tools that work with power tools (turning chisels, for example).

Interlocked-Grained Wood: Grain in which the fibers for several years slope in a right-handed direction, then for a number of years reverse to a left-handed direction, later change back to a righthanded pitch, and so on.

Jig: Any device acting as a guide for handwork or machine work.

Jointing: Gluing together narrow boards to make wider boards.

Kerf: Gap left as a saw makes a cut.

Kickback: The result of work fed into a machine too quickly, too slowly, or otherwise incorrectly, or work not controlled as it passes through. Kickback is usually violent and the piece, flung back towards the operator, is dangerous.

Kiln: A chamber having controlled air-flow, temperature, and relative humidity for drying lumber, veneer, and other wood products. Speeds drying of wood, as well as reducing the actual moisture content below what air-drying provides.

Kiln Dry: Wood that has been brought a controlled moisture content, usually 10% or less.

Knob: The front handle of a hand plane.

Knock-Down: Furniture that has been designed and built to be easily assembled and disassembled.

Knot: Portion of a branch or limb that has been surrounded by subsequent growth of the stem. The shape of the knot as it appears on a cut surface depends on the angle of the cut relative to the long axis of the knot.

Lacquer: Hard varnish once derived from tree sap. Today, nitrocellulose is used, as are polyester and polyurethane.

Linseed Oil: Product of crushed flax seeds. Drying oil, dries much faster when "boiled" (has chemical driers added).

Lumber: Product of the saw and planing mill not further manufactured than by sawing, resawing, passing lengthwise through a standard planing machine, crosscutting to length, or matching.

Luthier: A person who makes stringed instruments.

Mallet: Wooden-headed tool designed to drive cutting tools—chisels among others—with minimal damage to the cutting tool handle.

Mandrel: Revolving spindle of a lathe or other tool.

Marking Gauge: Adjustable tool to allow a straight line to be drawn at a set distance from a board's edge. May use a pin or roller blade marker.

Marking Knife: Used to give a very accurate mark. Bevel ground on one side of the blade only gives the most consistent accuracy.

Marquetry: Decorative inlay done in veneer.

MDF: Medium-Density Fiberboard. Uniformly consistent manmade board that comes in many styles today, and offers a good substrate for veneers and laminates.

Medullary Rays: Rays that radiate from the pith of a tree. They give a characteristic appearance to quarter-sawn oak.

Mineral Spirits: Petroleum distillate used as a replacement solvent for turpentine.

Miter: Joint formed by an intersection of two boards cut at angles other than 90°.

Miter Box: A box used with a saw to enable accurate cutting of miter joint angles.

Miter Square: Similar to a try square, with a blade fixed at 45° to the body.

Moisture Content: Amount of water contained in the wood, usually expressed as a percentage of the weight of the ovendry wood.

Molding (Moulding): A wood strip having a curved or projecting surface.

Molding Head: Round head for a table saw, designed to use several cutting blades (changeable) to produce small moldings.

Morse Taper: A gentle taper found at the top of drill press chucks, lathe chucks. Provides a centered, secure fit when properly installed.

Mortise: Female part of a mortise-and-tenon joint, slot cut into a wood member.

Mortise Gauge: A marking tool with two pins to mark each side of a mortise.

Nominal Size: The size of lumber before it is planed.

Old Growth: Timber in or from a mature, established forest.

Open-Grained Wood: Woods with large pores, such as mahogany, oak, ash, chestnut, and walnut. Also known as coarse-textured.

Open Life: The maximum time a glue remains viable once air is introduced.

Orbital Sander: Often called a block or finish sander, usually takes a quarter sheet of abrasive paper, gives a fine finish right up to edges.

Ovendry: Lumber dried in a kiln.

Overarm Router: Router in a fixed platform that works from above the table and workpieces.

Paraffin Wax: Used with bees wax to drop cost of mixed wax.

Peck: Pockets or areas of disintegrated wood caused by advanced stages of localized decay in the living tree. It is usually associated with cypress and incense cedar. Peck stops once the lumber is seasoned.

Pinch Dog: Double-spiked end clamp that is driven into end grain to hold boards together.

Pitch: The angle at which a plane iron meets the work.

Pitch Pocket: Opening extending parallel to the annual growth rings, containing pitch.

Plane: Body with a cutting iron for shaping the surface of wood.

Planed: Brought to smoothness with hand or power plane.

Plug: Piece of wood used to fill a hole in wood. Usually follows a counterbore that allows a screwhead to drop below the surface.

Plunge Router: Router with a plunging action that allows the bit to be lowered into the work at a controlled pace to a controlled depth.

Plywood: Glued wood panel made up of thin layers of veneer with the grain of adjacent layers at right angles, or of veneer in combination with a core of lumber or reconstituted wood. Most types have an odd number of layers.

Pocket Screws: Screws placed in specially drilled, slanted holes to assemble face frames and other cabinet parts.

Polyvinyl Acetate Adhesive (PVA): White glue, used cold, not waterproof and only minimally water resistant in most formulations.

Pounce Wheel: Metal handled wheel with a wheel on an axle at one end. The wheel has sharp teeth around its rim and is run along lines on plans that are placed on the material. The resulting pockmarked line is dusted with chalk, which produces a distinctive cut mark line on the wood.

Pulley: Device that works with a belt, or belts, to transmit power from a motor to a machine, basically a wheel grooved around its circumference. Set with blocks they help to reduce effort needed to lift heavy loads.

Push Stick: Stick with a notched end used to push stock through a saw blade when the hand would otherwise come too close.

Rabbet (U.K. Rebate): Ledge cut into the edge of a board.

Racking: A type of stress that produces shear or that produces tension at the top of a joint and compression at the bottom of a joint.

Radial Grain: Coincident with a radius from the axis of the tree or log to the circumference. A radial section is a lengthwise section in a plane that passes through the centerline of the tree trunk.

Raised Panel: Panel inserted in a frame in cabinetry or furniture, with a raised field.

Rake: The set of saw teeth.

Raker Tooth: A tooth in circular and band saw blades whose purpose is to clear chips or sawdust from the kerf.

Rays: Strips of cells extending radially within a tree and varying in height from a few cells in some species to 4" or more in oak. The rays store food and transport it in the tree. On quarter-sawn oak, the rays form a conspicuous figure.

Reaction Wood: Wood formed in parts of leaning and crooked stems and in branches. In hardwoods this is tension wood and in softwoods is compression wood.

Resin: A gum made by distilling pure turpentine from pine trees. Soluble in mineral spirits, alcohol, or turpentine. Not soluble in water.

Rip Saw: Hand or other saw designed to cut with the grain of wood.

Rise: The height of a stair.

Riser: Board on edge, usually plumb, that supports the front of the tread.

Rough Lumber: Lumber that has not been dressed (surfaced) but which has been sawn, edged, and trimmed.

RPM: Revolutions per minute of a machine or motor.

Run: The measurement of the horizontal plane of a stair.

Sapwood: Pale colored wood near the outside of the log. Sapwood is more disposed to decay than heartwood.

Scrub Plane: Single cutter metal plane with rounded edges on the cutter, used for the first planing of rough wood.

Seasoning: Removing moisture from green wood to improve its serviceability.

Set Time: The length of time an adhesive takes to cure enough to allow removal of clamps.

Shake: A separation along the grain, the greater part of which occurs between the rings of annual growth.

Shaper: Powered tool to produce molding. In the U.K., a spindle molder.

Shooting Board: A device to aid in planing the edges of thin wood.

Silex: Silicon oxide used to make paste grain fillers.

Silica: Flinty mineral in wood that creates difficulty when working.

Skip Plane: Fast planing job that leaves skips of cleared material, so gives some insight into the actual appearance of the wood's finished surface.

Softwoods: One of the botanical groups of trees with needlelike leaves, the conifers. Also the wood produced by such trees. Also known as non-porous woods. The term has little reference to the actual hardness of the wood.

Sole: The bottom surface (i.e., a plane's sole).

Spalt: Wood that has started to decay, presenting a different and often attractive figure.

Specific Gravity: The ratio of the ovendry weight of a sample to the weight of a volume of water equal to the volume of the sample at a specified moisture content (green, air-dry, or ovendry).

Spike Knot: Knot cut parallel to its long axis so that the exposed section is elongated.

Spiral-Grained Wood: Wood in which the fibers take a spiral course about the trunk of a tree.

Spline: Long, thin strip of wood used to add strength to joints. Currently, almost replaced by biscuit (plate) joinery.

Stain: A discoloration in wood caused by micro-organisms, metal, or chemicals. Also, materials used to deliberately impart color to wood.

Steel Wool: Used in three or four grades for wood finishing, usually to remove gloss from new finishes (0000 grade) or to remove a layer of finish (00 or 000 grades).

Stickers: Strips or boards used to separate the layers of lumber in a pile to improve air circulation. Inserted at regular intervals, from 18" to 36" depending on board thickness.

Stop: Device for stopping a cut or other action.

Straight-Grained Wood: Wood in which the fibers run parallel to the axis of a piece.

Stropping: Using a leather belt or wood block with leather glued on to finish hone a tool edge.

Structural Lumber: Lumber for use where specific strength properties are required.

Surfaced Lumber: Lumber dressed by running it through a planer.

Synthetic Adhesive: Any adhesive not made from natural (usually animal) substances.

Tailstock: Movable head of a lathe.

Tangential Grain: Occurs when the surface of a board is cut perpendicular to the log's radius. The annual rings create arches on the face of the board.

TCG: Triple chip grind. Configuration for tip grind on circular saw blades, used for multiple materials, very smooth cuts.

Template (Templet): A stand-off that allows a cut made to a pattern.

Tenon: A projection at the end of a wood part, inserted into a mortise to make a mortise-and-tenon joint.

Tenon Saws: Small back saws designed to cut tenons.

Texture: Term used interchangeably with grain. Combines density and degree of contrast between earlywood and latewood.

Tool Rest: Movable tool support device on a lathe.

Toothing Plane: Plane with toothed blade for scoring a surface for better glue adhesion during veneering.

Tote: The rear handle of a hand plane.

Trammel: A beam compass.

Trunnion: Arched structure that supports the tilting motor/arbor/blade assembly on band saws, table saws, scroll saws and similar tools. The actual load on the trunnions varies from tool to tool, and in types within tools, but the sturdier they are, and the higher quality material they are made from, the better (cast iron is usually considered best).

Try Square: Used for marking and testing wood. Sized

Vacuum Press: For veneering large work. Atmospheric pressure pushes down the veneer.

Veneer: Thin wood used over a substrate to enhance appearance.

Veneer Matching: Matching veneer patterns to produce a particular design or look.

Veneer Saw: Small saw with a curved edge that doesn't dig in.

Warp: Any variation from a true or plane surface. Warp includes bow, crook, cup, and twist, or any combination.

Wavy-Grained Wood: Wood in which the fibers take the form of waves or undulations.

Wedging: With mortise-and-tenon joints, through tenons are split and wedges are applied through, under, above, or at the end.

GLOSSARY & INDEX

Glossary & Index

Acknowledgments

As always, thanks to my wife, Frances, for keeping most of the world at bay long enough for me to finish this book.

The list of people who have supplied information, photos, and gear for my photography is long, and I am very grateful to each and every one. Rob Lee at Lee Valley let me get my hands on some of their wonderful planes with time to learn a bit about them, as well as helping in other areas. Dave Warren, an old friend and U.S. distributor for E. C. Emmerich hand planes, supplied tools and expertise generously. Mark Cross at HTC was particularly helpful, as always. Ken Kueter and Mike Mangan helped with information on Craftsman tools. I'd also like to thank Lisa Agostini of Freud. Leigh Bailey at Hitachi helped greatly, as did Jason Feldner at Bosch, and Chad Corley from Weber Shandwick for Delta and Porter-Cable. Steve Knight supplied one of his great handmade planes for use in a couple of photographs. Stanley Tools, through Ryan Murphy at Mullen PR, helped, as did CooperTools (Lufkin, Plumb, Crescent) through Keith Hobbs (Business Services Associates).

Plenty of general encouragement came from Dale Toms, Tom Watson, and Bobby Weaver, three good friends.

And, in advance, I apologize to anyone I missed.

The publisher would like to thank Woodcraft and Rockler for supplying many of the photos in this book. Special thanks to Steve Latta, Paul Meisel, and John Nelson for their input and expertise.

Credits

Photographs and illustrations courtesy Hardwood Information Center: p. 40, p. 41.

Illustration courtesy Hardwood Association: p. 38.

Photographs courtesy Woodcraft Supply Corporation: p. 6, pp. 78–79 (all), p. 80 (top & bottom), p. 87, p. 88 (second, third, fourth, & fifth), p. 89 (third and fourth), p. 90 (top three), p. 91 (second & third), p. 93 (all), p. 98 (top three), p. 99 (top three & bottom), p. 100 (bottom three), p. 103 (middle two), p. 112 (top), p. 115, p. 125 (bottom), p. 127, p. 145 (all), p. 146 (all), p. 147, p. 148 (all), p. 149 (all), p. 150 (top), p. 152, p. 155, p. 156, p. 164 (all), p. 165 (all).

Photographs and illustrations courtesy McFeely's: p. 49, p. 54 (bottom two), p. 55 (all), p. 56 (all), p. 58, p. 61 (all), p. 64–66.

Photographs courtesy Sears: p. 52, p. 129, p. 188 (top).

Photographs and illustrations courtesy Ridgid: p. 114 (bottom), p. 126, p. 194 (all).

Photographs courtesy Rockler: p. 63 (bottom), p. 89 (first and second), p. 91 (top).

Photographs courtesy Lee Valley Tools Ltd.: p. 90 (bottom), p. 94 (top four), p. 95 (top).

Photograph courtesy Stanley: p. 92 (bottom).

Photographs courtesy Delta Machinery: p. 105, p. 113 (bottom), p. 114 (top two), p. 123, p. 128, p. 130, p. 150 (bottom).

Photograph courtesy SawStop: p. 186 (bottom).

Photographs courtesy Bosch: p. 89 (bottom), p. 106 (top), p. 109 (bottom), p. 111 (bottom), p. 119, p. 133, p. 134 (bottom).

Photographs courtesy *Scroll Saw Workshop***:** p. 110 (all).

Photographs courtesy Creative Commons: p. 62 (top; courtesy Sh4rp_i), p. 62 (bottom; courtesy cheryl.reed). Photos used under the Creative Commons Attribution 2.0 Generic (CC BY 2.0) license. To learn more, visit www.creativecommons.org/licenses.

Photograph courtesy Festool: p. 121.

Photographs courtesy Chris Gleason: p. 7 (top), p. 63 (top), p. 112 (bottom), p. 113 (middle).

Credits

Photographs courtesy Ryobi Tools: p. 107, p. 124.

Photographs courtesy Milwaukee Electric Tools: p. 101 (all), p. 108 (bottom), p. 111 (top).

Photograph courtesy Craftsman: p. 134 (top).

Photograph courtesy General Tools: p. 91 (fourth).

Photograph courtesy Forest Products Lab: p. 33 (bottom).

Photograph courtesy Grizzly Industrial: p. 88 (bottom).

Photographs courtesy Dremel: p. 95 (middle), p. 108 (top).

Photograph courtesy *American Woodworker***:** p. 7 (bottom).

Photograph courtesy Wagner SprayTech: p. 172.

Photograph courtesy Porter-Cable: p. 143. The PORTER CABLE® name and logo and the gray and black color scheme, ✦ "four point star" design, and three contrasting/outlined longitudinal stripes are trademarks of PORTER CABLE, used with permission.

Photograph courtesy Makita: p. 113 (top).